TWENTY GERMAN POETS

A BILINGUAL COLLECTION

Edited, Translated, and Introduced by

WALTER KAUFMANN

THE MODERN LIBRARY · NEW YORK

The Editor wishes to acknowledge with gratitude the permission of the following publishers to reprint in this book materials controlled by them:

Verlag Helmut Küpper, Munich: for the poetry of Stefan George.

S. Fischer Verlag, Frankfurt am Main: for the poetry of Hugo von Hofmannsthal and Franz Werfel.

R. Piper et Co. Verlag, Munich: for the epigrams of Christian Morgenstern.

Insel-Verlag, Frankfurt am Main: for the poetry of Christian Morgenstern and Rainer Maria Rilke.

Otto Müller Verlag, Salzburg: for the poetry of Georg Trakl.

Limes-Verlag, Wiesbaden: for the poetry of Gottfried Benn.

Phaidon Press, London: for the poetry of Klabund.

Atrium Verlag, London: for the poetry of Erich Kästner.

Suhrkamp Verlag, Frankfurt am Main: for the poetry of Hermann Hesse.

THE MODERN LIBRARY

is published by

RANDOM HOUSE, INC.

Manufactured in the United States of America

For

Dinah

ACKNOWLEDGMENTS

Many of these poems I translated initially to be able to share them with my wife, Hazel. This book developed from our dialogue, and in the final stage our children, Dinah and David—no longer children—participated. I am also grateful to Alan Pearlman and Felix Kaufmann for helpful criticisms.

CONTENTS

INTRODUCTION

Strictly speaking, this volume is not an anthology—a collection of blossoms. There are places from which one does not bring home flowers to show what one has seen.

On the eve of the Second World War, many men of good will said that they could not understand how the great "people of poets and thinkers" could have produced the realities of the thirties. The legend gained popularity that there were two kinds of Germans, two different traditions, one good and one bad.

The excessive aestheticism of some anthologies abets such notions. One picks pretty sentiments from Heine's early poems, possibly also from Goethe's, emphasizes the romantics' lyric flights, concentrates on nostalgia and unhappy love, ignores everything in Goethe and Heine that bites, leaves out Nietzsche and George's later verse, and stops with Rilke. My point in including many previously untranslated poems is not a mere desire for novelty and least of all the wish to indict any poet: rather, this selection should facilitate a better understanding of German poetry.

The English word "poetry" comes from the Greek word for making. And much English poetry is indeed make-believe, contrivance, a world apart. The "metaphysical" poets fashioned far-fetched images, so-called conceits. Milton, Blake, and Yeats contrived mythological worlds of their own; the romantics, poses. Gradually it came to be felt widely that poetry is remote from life, and that whatever can be understood without much study can hardly be good poetry.

There are at least two types of esotericism. The first erects barriers that study alone can surmount. The second requires experience to be understood. Each is obviously compatible with good verse as well as bad; and so are poems difficult in both ways. But it is worth noting that opaqueness that demands glosses is no warrant of profundity, and that much of the best German verse does not call for any commentary.

The German word for "poem," *Gedicht,* comes from *dicht,* which means dense. The poet or *Dichter* is a condenser, and many of the most renowned German poems are indeed pithy and pregnant rather than make-believe. Three types of verse have been cultivated far more by the best German poets than by the most celebrated English poets since Shakespeare: straightforward outbursts, poetic mainly in their concentrated power; light verse offering serious thoughts and often acid criticism; and *Spruch-Dichtung,* epigrammatic verse. By omitting the last two genres and toning down the first, one can assimilate German to English poetry and give a highly misleading picture: that now current. The selections that follow do not go to the opposite extreme. The aim is rather to create a characteristic image.

In the English-speaking world, the gap between the spoken language and poetic convention had become so great by the end of the Victorian era that some twentieth-century poets have gone to extremes to overcome it. By contrast, most of the best German poems had always stayed surprisingly close to the spoken language. Not only Heine, Meyer, and Nietzsche are cases in point, but even much of Goethe's, Schiller's, and Hölderlin's verse. As a result, Rilke did not face the problems confronting Eliot, but could write in an idiom that is at the same time strikingly poetic and extremely close to good prose.

Translators who consider it part of their job to transpose all they touch into whatever they consider either "poetic" or the peculiar idiom of the twentieth century are bound to miss points like this; and this is even more obviously true of those who merely use foreign poems as a point of departure, feeling free to "adapt." It is one of the most unusual features of the translations that follow that they have all been made by a single translator; and they might therefore be expected to resemble each other rather closely in tone. My aim has been, on the contrary, to make the translations extremely faithful, not only in meaning but also in tone.

Goethe should sound like Goethe, Heine like Heine, Rilke like Rilke, and Kästner like Kästner. Even readers with little or no German should be able to feel what distinguishes

Rilke's poetry, to what extent Kästner resembles Heine, where Goethe was "romantic" and where he was "modern," or how Klabund's re-creations of Chinese poems introduce a new note. It is for this reason, not for the sake of any pedantry, that I have generally followed the original meters and rhymes. The reader should be in a position to note—in the translations, too—the differences in tone even between the young Goethe and the old Goethe, or the early and the late Rilke.

If some of my English versions are much more poetic than others, and some not poetic at all, that in itself is not necessarily a measure of success and failure: the same differences may exist between the originals, which are printed on facing pages.

No poem has been included merely as a matter of obligation: all the German poems that follow strike me as very interesting. But that does not mean, of course, that I like all of them equally well. My own favorites include Goethe's "Prometheus" and "Blessed Yearning," Hölderlin's "To the Parcae," Meyer's "Roman Fountain," Rilke's "Love Song," "Panther," "Archaic Torso," "Leda," and also his late poems. But a collection like that, even if doubled or tripled in size, would not give anything approximately a representative picture of German poetry; least of all could it tell the story that the pages that follow are meant to tell.

The sequence of the poets, and of the poems by each poet, is roughly chronological. Precision in this matter is impossible because Goethe, for example, outlived several younger poets; many good poets have been contemporaries; and the dates of the individual poems are not always known. Poems by the same poet have always been kept together, arranged as far as possible to reflect his development; and poets who made their mark earlier have generally been placed before those who published later.

Even so, there are gaps in our story. Some of these are filled in the prefaces that precede the selections from every poet. Of course, no history of German literature could be attempted in this compass, nor even a discussion of all the poems included. But some particularly relevant information is provided, and a few allusions are explained.

No suggestion whatsoever is intended that poems omitted here are necessarily inferior to all those included, or even that all the poets represented here are superior to all the rest. To give the most obvious example, many German poets have written better verse than Dahn's; and yet the one poem by Dahn that appears in this volume strikes a note that is in some ways more important—and less dispensable—than the addition of a few more poems that resemble Eichendorff's "The Hermit," without quite equaling Eichendorff's superb simplicity. And precisely in Dahn's case it seems essential to stay close to the rhythm of the original, lest one falsify the mood. Nietzsche's "To the Mistral" is another poem that depends utterly on its rhythm; and the same seems to me to be true, if not quite so obviously, of Rilke's late poems. The popular notion that one can keep the tone even if one changes meaning and meter, substituting free verse for rhymed stanzas and introducing rhymes where there are none in the original, is surely false. What is perhaps true is that in translating poetry from some other languages into English the tone of the original cannot be preserved. In this respect, however, translating German is happily easier than rendering some other tongues into English.

Strictly speaking—to repeat it once more—this volume is not an anthology but aims to be a book of one piece. A few of the translations were made as much as twenty years ago and only slightly revised recently; many more were made this past summer. But much that was done off and on over the past twenty years was left out, and a good deal was done in recent months because it seemed to me to belong in this volume. The reader should not look upon this book as a meadow in which he might pick a few flowers here and there, but rather as a path that leads into the mountains and gradually offers a view.

W. K.

Princeton,
November 25, 1961

JOHANN WOLFGANG VON GOETHE

(1749-1832)

Goethe, who coined the word *Weltliteratur* (world literature), was the first German poet to find a world-wide audience during his lifetime. His early novel, *Die Leiden des jungen Werthers* (1774, The Sufferings of Young Werther) was an international success. His later novels and his plays also won wide respect from the start; and his *Faust* (*A Fragment,* 1790; *Part One,* 1808) was immediately regarded as the most ambitious and significant German drama. Goethe was a scientist and a statesman too, and approximated the Renaissance ideal of the universal man.

None of his achievements, however, rival the popularity of his poems. His rank as Germany's greatest poet is as secure as Shakespeare's claim to being England's outstanding dramatist. Not only literary historians, teachers, and the German people generally are agreed on this: almost all subsequent German poets have looked on Goethe as a titan; even those, like Novalis, Heine, and Nietzsche, who were occasionally sharply critical of him.

Of the poems that follow, a few may require some comments. "Prometheus" was written as part of a play by the same name; but the play remained a fragment. The poem was first printed by F. H. Jacobi in his anonymously published book, *Ueber die Lehre des Spinoza* (1785, On the Teaching of Spinoza). The crux of this volume was that Lessing, the great German poet and critic, was said to have avowed his Spinozism shortly before his death in 1781; and "Spinozism" was then considered a euphemism for atheism. On page 11, Jacobi reported a conversation in which he had said to Lessing: "Here is a poem: you have often *given* offense; now it is your turn to *take* it for once." At this point a footnote follows—or rather two footnotes, depending on the edition. (I have a copy in which there are two pages 11, one with the one footnote, the other with the alternative.) One footnote reads: "See the poem at the end . . ." The other footnote says: "This poem, which attacks all providence in very harsh terms, cannot be printed here, for good reasons." A postscript at the end of the book informs the reader: "The poem 'Prometheus' is to be inserted between pages 48 and 49. It has been printed separately [without page numbers], so anybody who would rather not have it in his copy need not have it there. And another consideration, too, has led me to adopt this procedure. It is not altogether impossible that my volume might be confiscated here or there on account of 'Prometheus.' I am hoping that in such places one will be satisfied to remove only the punishable separate pages. When the poem is left out, pages 11 and 12 are cut out and the alternative pages are substituted."

After he had read the poem, Lessing said, "as he gave it back to me: I did not take offense; I have long had this firsthand. I: You know the poem? Lessing: The poem I had not read before, but I find it good. I: In its own way I do, too; otherwise I should not have shown it to you. Lessing: I do not mean that. The point of view expressed in this poem is my own point of view. Orthodox conceptions of the deity are no longer for me; I cannot endure them. *Hen kai pan* [One and All]! I know nothing else. That is where this poem points, too. And I must confess, I like it very much. I: Then you would seem to agree pretty much with Spinoza. Lessing: If I had to name my outlook after anyone, I could not think of a better name."

The following year, Jacobi published, under his own name, a reply to Moses Mendelssohn's attack on his volume, insisting that he was right about Lessing's agreement with Spinoza; the polemic continued; and in 1789 a second revised edition of the original volume appeared. These polemics gradually led to the rehabilitation of Spinoza's name, chiefly at the hands of Fichte, Schelling, and Hegel. Ever since, Spinoza has been generally acclaimed as one of the greatest philosophers of all time, and knowledge of his works has grown to the point where Goethe's "Prometheus" no longer strikes us as particularly "Spinozistic." Its mood is quite different from Spinoza's *Ethics* with its celebrated geometric method. Brief and powerful, it may well be one of the greatest poems of all time: a truly classical statement.

Even as this poem transcends Prometheus' defiance of Zeus, "Ganymede" does not merely deal with the story in which Zeus, in the form of an eagle, carried off a youth to whom he had taken a fancy. It is a harbinger of romanticism. To do justice to "Ganymede," one has to keep in mind that, like "Prometheus" and "Reviewer," it was written in the early seventeen-seventies, more than twenty years before Keats was born. (Wordsworth was born in 1770, Shelley in 1792, Keats in 1795.)

Goethe was decidedly a revolutionary who spurned the styles perfected by others. Before a group of poets in Germany called itself "romantic," in part to distinguish itself from Goethe's and Schiller's "classicism," Goethe himself had long mocked the weaknesses of romanticism through the mouth of Mephistopheles, in *Faust.*

"Scared Hesitation" and the poem addressed to Charlotte von Stein were written in the late seventies. Frau von Stein (1742–1827), the wife of a functionary at the Weimar court, was one of the most important women in Goethe's life; and their correspondence has been published in two volumes. The heroine of Goethe's *Iphigenie* (1787) is a highly idealized portrait of her in the role of sister—a notion alluded to in the poem translated here.

Johann Kaspar Lavater (1741–1801), ridiculed in the next poem, was a minister in Zurich and is remembered chiefly for his studies of physiognomy. Mignon is a figure in Goethe's novel, *Wilhelm Meister,* which was originally published in installments (1795ff.); but her song, like the three poems preceding it, was written during the eighties. The song of the Harp Player is also from *Wilhelm Meister.*

Tasso (1790), like *Iphigenie,* has only five dramatis personae; and these two plays mark the culmination of Goethe's so-called classicism. For all their "classical" restraint, however, many scholars, especially outside Germany, consider some of the works of this period "romantic." Indeed, Goethe himself is occasionally classified as a romantic, although he identified the classical with the healthy and the romantic with the sick, and juxtaposed Tasso with Antonio.

To avoid misunderstanding him, one must remember that Goethe was never quite like his Faust; that he always was Mephistopheles, too. In a selection from his poems, this point is probably best made by offering some of his *Venetian Epigrams* (1790), including several that are still omitted in almost all editions—as Jacobi might have said, "for good reasons." The point is not to give offense but to create a true image of Goethe. When he has not been pictured as a romantic, he has often been presented as an "Olympian" incarnation of propriety, if not downright stuffiness. In fact, he never bowed to convention in what truly mattered to him. Beethoven's celebrated refusal to take a bow when the duke's party passed seemed silly to Goethe—as did Beethoven's lecturing him on his behavior toward Bettina von Arnim who had publicly quarreled with Goethe's wife at a time when Weimar society spurned her. Goethe and Christiane Vulpius had married only when their son, August, was seventeen.

Some of the *Epigrams* were first published in 1915; but for any discussion of the history of style and of Goethe's modernity they are all relevant. In the most complete German edition, edited by Dr. Otto Deneke (Berlin, Hyperionverlag, no date, limited edition of 1200 copies), the epigrams that follow bear the numbers: 13, 19, 20, 25, 26, 30, 69, 77, 81, 89, 96, 105, 111a, 115, 119, 120, and 136. In the last edition of Goethe's works that was published under his supervision, the so-called *Ausgabe letzter Hand*, Vol. I (1827), the numbers are different, and several of those offered here are missing: 11, —, —, —, 12, 15, —, 52, —, —, —, 66, —, 73, —, —, 88. In that edition there were 103 epigrams in all, while the Deneke volume contains 158. The reason for including so many that the poet himself did not, and could not, publish is, to say it once more briefly, to document the Mephistophelian side of Goethe.

"Nearness of Her Lover" was written in the nineties; so were many of Goethe's best ballads, which are not included in this volume. I particularly admire "The God and the Bayadère" and "The Pariah"; but both of these ballads are exceedingly long.

The old Goethe cultivated two new kinds of verse. His attempts to present ultimate wisdom in rhymes are here represented by the first and probably best of his five "Orphic" stanzas, each of which bears a Greek name. They were written in 1817. The other new path he struck led to a whole volume of verse, published in 1819 when he was seventy: *West-Östlicher Divan* (West-Eastern Divan). Here he paid homage to Persian poetry, especially to the fourteenth-century poet Hafiz. Later, such poets as Friedrich Rückert (1788–1866) and August Graf Platen-Hallermünde (1796–1835) followed in Goethe's wake and became virtuosos in Oriental forms. "Blessed Yearning" is a wisdom poem from the *Divan*, and generally acknowledged to be one of several gems from that collection.

My translation of "Blessed Yearning" was first published in my *Critique of Religion and Philosophy* (Section 7), where the image of the butterfly, in a context in which one would expect a moth, is discussed. A similar image is used in the first selection from *Tasso*. My *From Shakespeare to Existentialism* contains four chapters on Goethe, including one on "Goethe versus Romanticism."

PROMETHEUS

Bedecke deinen Himmel, Zeus,
Mit Wolkendunst
Und übe, dem Knaben gleich,
Der Disteln köpft,
An Eichen dich und Bergeshöhn;
Musst mir meine Erde
Doch lassen stehn
Und meine Hütte, die du nicht gebaut,
Und meinen Herd,
Um dessen Glut
Du mich beneidest.

Ich kenne nichts Ärmeres
Unter der Sonn als euch, Götter!
Ihr nähret kümmerlich
Von Opfersteuern
Und Gebetshauch
Eure Majestät
Und darbtet, wären
Nicht Kinder und Bettler
Hoffnungsvolle Toren.

Da ich ein Kind war,
Nicht wusste, wo aus noch ein,
Kehrt ich mein verirrtes Auge
Zur Sonne, als wenn drüber wär
Ein Ohr, zu hören meine Klage,
Ein Herz wie meins,
Sich des Bedrängten zu erbarmen.

PROMETHEUS

Cover your heavens, Jove,
with misty clouds
and practice, like a boy
beheading thistles,
on oaks and mountain peaks!
My earth you must leave me
still standing,
and my cottage, which you did not build,
and my hearth
whose warmth
you envy me.

I know nothing poorer
under the sun than you gods!
Wretchedly you nourish
your majesty
on sacrificial tolls
and flimsy prayers,
and would starve if children
and beggars were not
hopeful fools.

When I was a child,
not knowing my way,
I turned my erring eyes
sunward, as if above there were
an ear to hear my lamentation,
a heart like mine
to care for the distressed.

Wer half mir
Wider der Titanen Übermut?
Wer rettete vom Tode mich,
Von Sklaverei?
Hast du nicht alles selbst vollendet,
Heilig glühend Herz?
Und glühtest jung und gut,
Betrogen, Rettungsdank
Dem Schlafenden da droben?

Ich dich ehren? Wofür?
Hast du die Schmerzen gelindert
Je des Beladenen?
Hast du die Tränen gestillet
Je des Geängsteten?
Hat nicht mich zum Manne geschmiedet
Die allmächtige Zeit
Und das ewige Schicksal,
Meine Herrn und deine?

Wähntest du etwa,
Ich sollte das Leben hassen,
In Wüsten fliehen,
Weil nicht alle
Blütenträume reiften?

Hier sitz ich, forme Menschen
Nach meinem Bilde,
Ein Geschlecht, das mir gleich sei,
Zu leiden, zu weinen,
Zu geniessen und zu freuen sich,
Und dein nicht zu achten,
Wie ich!

Who helped me
against the Titans' wanton insolence?
Who rescued me from death,
from slavery?
Have you not done all this yourself,
my holy glowing heart?
And young and good, you glowed,
betrayed, with thanks for rescue
to him who slept above.

I honor you? For what?
Have you ever eased the suffering
of the oppressed?
Have you ever stilled the tears
of the frightened?
Was I not welded to manhood
by almighty Time
and eternal Fate,
my masters and yours?

Did you fancy perchance
that I should hate life
and fly to the desert
because not all
by blossom dreams ripened?

Here I sit, forming men
in my own image,
a race to be like me,
to suffer, to weep,
to delight and to rejoice,
and to defy you,
as I do.

GANYMED

Wie im Morgenglanze
Du rings mich anglühst,
Frühling, Geliebter!
Mit tausendfacher Liebeswonne
Sich an mein Herz drängt
Deiner ewigen Wärme
Heilig Gefühl,
Unendliche Schöne!

Dass ich dich fassen möcht'
In diesen Arm!

Ach, an deinem Busen
Lieg ich, schmachte,
Und deine Blumen, dein Gras
Drängen sich an mein Herz.
Du kühlst den brennenden
Durst meines Busens,
Lieblicher Morgenwind!
Ruft drein die Nachtigall
Liebend nach mir aus dem Nebeltal.

Ich komm, ich komme!
Wohin? Ach, wohin?

Hinauf! Hinauf strebt's.
Es schweben die Wolken
Abwärts, die Wolken
Neigen sich der sehnenden Liebe.

GANYMEDE

How in morning splendor
you glow at me,
Spring, my beloved!
With thousandfold loving caresses
your eternal warmth's
holy feeling
surges toward my heart,
infinite beauty!

That I might welcome you
in this arm!

Ah, at your bosom
I lie and languish,
and your flowers and grass
surge toward my heart.
You cool the burning
thirst of my bosom,
lovely wind of the morning!
Out of the misty vale
the loving nightingale calls me.

I come, I am coming!
Whither? Ah, whither?

Up! Up it strives.
The clouds are floating
downwards, the clouds are
coming to meet my love's longing.

Mir! Mir!
In euerm Schosse
Aufwärts!
Umfangend umfangen!
Aufwärts an deinen Busen,
All liebender Vater!

REZENSENT

Da hatt ich einen Kerl zu Gast,
Er war mir eben nicht zur Last;
Ich hatt just mein gewöhnlich Essen,
Hat sich der Kerl pumpsatt gefressen,
Zum Nachtisch, was ich gespeichert hatt.
Und kaum ist mir der Kerl so satt,
Tut ihn der Teufel zum Nachbar führen,
Über mein Essen zu räsonnieren:
Die Supp hätt können gewürzter sein,
Der Braten brauner, firner der Wein.
Der Tausendsackerment!
Schlagt ihn tot, den Hund! Es ist ein Rezensent.

Mine! Mine!
In your lap
upwards!
Embracing, embraced!
Upwards towards your bosom,
All-loving Father!

REVIEWER

A fellow came to dine with me,
I did not mind his company:
I had my customary dinner,
he gorged himself, did not grow thinner,
and then he drank many a cup.
When he is thoroughly filled up,
the devil moves him to drop in next door,
where the rascal feels called upon to deplore
that the soup did not have quite enough spice,
and the roast was too rare, and the wine not nice.
Filth, fire, and manure!
Beat him to death! The dog is a reviewer.

[FEIGER GEDANKEN]

Feiger Gedanken
Bängliches Schwanken,
Weibisches Zagen,
Ängstliches Klagen
Wendet kein Elend,
Macht dich nicht frei.

Allen Gewalten
Zum Trutz sich erhalten;
Nimmer sich beugen,
Kräftig sich zeigen,
Rufet die Arme
Der Götter herbei.

AN CHARLOTTE VON STEIN

Warum gabst du uns die tiefen Blicke,
Unsre Zukunft ahndungsvoll zu schaun,
Unsrer Liebe, unserm Erdenglücke
Wähnend selig nimmer hinzutraun?
Warum gabst uns, Schicksal, die Gefühle,
Uns einander in das Herz zu sehn,
Um durch all die seltenen Gewühle
Unser wahr Verhältnis auszuspähn?

FROM "LILA"

Scared hesitation,
procrastination,
womanish sighing,
cowardly crying
changes no odds
and makes you not free.

Standing upright
all powers to spite,
never submit,
prove yourself fit:
that will invoke
the aid of the gods.

TO CHARLOTTE VON STEIN

Why did you grant us the searching glance
that forebodes the future and, O Fate,
forbids blissful blindness, trust in chance?
Why did you grant eyes that penetrate
love and happiness and all illusion,
make us see the other's heart, inspect
every urge till through the strange confusion
our true relation we detect?

Ach, so viele tausend Menschen kennen,
Dumpf sich treibend, kaum ihr eigen Herz,
Schweben zwecklos hin und her und rennen
Hoffnungslos in unversehnen Schmerz;
Jauchzen wieder, wenn der schnellen Freuden
Unerwart'te Morgenröte tagt.
Nur uns armen liebevollen beiden
Ist das wechselseit'ge Glück versagt,
Uns zu lieben, ohn uns zu verstehen,
In dem andern sehn, was er nie war,
Immer frisch auf Traumglück auszugehen
Und zu schwanken auch in Traumgefahr.

Glücklich, den ein leerer Traum beschäftigt!
Glücklich, dem die Ahndung eitel wär'!
Jede Gegenwart und jeder Blick bekräftigt
Traum und Ahndung leider uns noch mehr.
Sag, was will das Schicksal uns bereiten?
Sag, wie band es uns so rein genau?
Ach du warst in abgelebten Zeiten
Meine Schwester oder meine Frau.

Kanntest jeden Zug in meinem Wesen,
Spähtest, wie die reinste Nerve klingt,
Konntest mich mit einem *Blicke lesen,*
Den so schwer ein sterblich Aug durchdringt.
Tropftest Mässigung dem heissen Blute,
Richtetest den wilden irren Lauf,
Und in deinen Engelsarmen ruhte
Die zerstörte Brust sich wieder auf;
Hieltest zauberleicht ihn angebunden
Und vergaukeltest ihm manchen Tag.

Thousands, drifting dully, scarcely know
their own hearts, are heedless of the morrow,
run, while blindly drifting to and fro,
hopeless into unexpected sorrow;
jubilate again when quick joys' tide
breaks like unexpected dawn above.
But such mutual pleasure is denied
to our wretched loving hearts: to love
each the other without understanding,
see the other as he never was,
tirelessly dreamlike bliss demanding,
dreading only an imagined cause.

Happy whom an empty dream oppressed,
who his vain forebodings can ignore!
Every presence, every glance attest
our dreams and dread forebodings more.
What plans our fate yet to bestow?
How were we so closely matched in life?
Ah, you were in times lived long ago
my beloved sister or my wife.

Every feature of my soul you knew,
felt if but the slightest nerve was sounded;
with a single glance you read me through,
whom no other mortal has expounded;
soothed the raging blood with measured charms,
straightened out its course, wild and insane,
and through rest in your angelic arms
was the ravaged breast restored again.
Lightly holding him with magic powers,
you would charm the pleasant days away.

Welche Seligkeit glich jenen Wonnestunden,
Da er dankbar dir zu Füssen lag,
Fühlt sein Herz an deinem Herzen schwellen,
Fühlte sich in deinem Auge gut,
Alle seine Sinnen sich erhellen
Und beruhigen sein brausend Blut!

Und von allem dem schwebt ein Erinnern
Nur noch um das ungewisse Herz,
Fühlt die alte Wahrheit ewig gleich im Innern,
Und der neue Zustand wird ihm Schmerz.
Und wir scheinen uns nur halb beseelet,
Dämmernd ist um uns der hellste Tag.
Glücklich, dass das Schicksal, das uns quälet,
Uns doch nicht verändern mag!

AUF LAVATERS LIED EINES CHRISTEN AN CHRISTUS

Du bist! du bist! sagt Lavater, Du bist!!
Du bist!!! du bist!!!! du bist Herr Jesus Christ!!!!!
Er wiederholte nicht so heftig Wort und Lehre,
Wenn es ganz just mit dieser Sache wäre.

And no bliss could equal those sweet hours
when at your feet gratefully he lay,
when he felt his heart at your heart swell,
all his brightened senses would increase,
when you looked at him his soul grew well
and his roaring blood at last found peace.

And of all this, reminiscence hovers
over our hearts' uncertainty;
the forgotten truth felt by the lovers
fills their present state with agony.
And we seem to be but half alive,
dusk around us is the brightest day.
Blessed that Fate, whatever it contrive,
cannot alter our way.

ON LAVATER'S SONG OF A CHRISTIAN TO CHRIST

"Thou art! Thou art!!" Lavater says. "Thou art!!
Thou art!!! Thou art!!!! Thou art, Christ our Lord!!!!!"
He would not be so violent in his repetition
if it were not a questionable proposition.

DER ERFAHRENE

ANTWORTEN BEI EINEM GESELLSCHAFTLICHEN FRAGESPIEL

Geh den Weibern zart entgegen:
Du gewinnst sie, auf mein Wort!
Und wer rasch ist und verwegen,
Kommt vielleicht noch besser fort.
Doch wem wenig dran gelegen
Scheinet, ob er reizt und rührt,
Der beleidigt, der verführt.

NACHTGEDANKEN

Euch bedaur ich, unglücksel'ge Sterne,
Die ihr schön seid und so herrlich scheinet,
Dem bedrängten Schiffer gerne leuchtet,
Unbelohnt von Göttern und von Menschen:
Denn ihr liebt nicht, kanntet nie die Liebe!
Unaufhaltsam führen ew'ge Stunden
Eure Reihen durch den weiten Himmel.
Welche Reise habt ihr schon vollendet,
Seit ich, weilend in dem Arm der Liebsten,
Euer und der Mitternacht vergessen!

THE VOICE OF EXPERIENCE

Meet women with tender bearing,
you will conquer them, I bet;
and the quick man who is daring
will perhaps do better yet;
but the man who seems uncaring
what response he may unloose
will offend and thus seduce.

THOUGHTS BY NIGHT

You I pity, miserable stars,
that are fair and shine so splendidly,
lend your light to distressed fishermen,
unrewarded both by men and gods;
for you love not, never knew what love is!
But relentlessly eternal hours
lead your legions through the far-flung heavens.
Ah, what journey have you just completed
since I, resting in my loved one's arms,
did not even think of you or midnight.

MIGNON

Heiss mich nicht reden, heiss mich schweigen,
Denn mein Geheimnis ist mir Pflicht;
Ich möchte dir mein ganzes Innre zeigen,
Allein das Schicksal will es nicht.

Zur rechten Zeit vertreibt der Sonne Lauf
Die finstre Nacht, und sie muss sich erhellen;
Der harte Fels schliesst seinen Busen auf,
Missgönnt der Erde nicht die tiefverborgnen Quellen.

Ein jeder sucht im Arm des Freundes Ruh,
Dort kann die Brust in Klagen sich ergiessen;
Allein ein Schwur drückt mir die Lippen zu,
Und nur ein Gott vermag sie aufzuschliessen.

HARFENSPIELER

Wer nie sein Brot mit Tränen ass,
Wer nie die kummervollen Nächte
Auf seinem Bette weinend sass,
Der kennt euch nicht, ihr himmlischen Mächte.

Ihr führt ins Leben uns hinein,
Ihr lasst den Armen schuldig werden,
Dann überlasst ihr ihn der Pein;
Denn alle Schuld rächt sich auf Erden.

MIGNON

Bid me not speak, bid me be still
because my secret is my writ;
to show you all my heart would be my will,
but fate does not permit.

In time dispels the sun's eternal course
the gloomy night, and it submits to dawn;
the rigid rock itself must burst perforce
that hidden wells break out into the thirsty lawn

In friend's embrace all agony is healed.
and weary souls can be restored to hope;
alas, an oath keeps my lips ever sealed,
and but a god has power to break them open.

THE HARP PLAYER'S SONG

Who never ate with tears his bread,
who never through night's grievous hours
sat sleepless, weeping on his bed,
he does not know you, heaven's powers.

You lead us into life's domain,
you catch the poor in guilt and dearth,
and then you leave him to his pain:
avenged is every guilt on earth.

TORQUATO TASSO FÜNFTER AUFZUG

AUS DEM ZWEITEN AUFTRITT

Wenn ich nicht sinnen oder dichten soll,
So ist das Leben mir kein Leben mehr.
Verbiete du dem Seidenwurm, zu spinnen,
Wenn er sich schon dem Tode näher spinnt:
Das köstliche Geweb entwickelt er
Aus seinem Innersten, und lässt nicht ab,
Bis er in seinen Sarg sich eingeschlossen.
O geb ein guter Gott uns auch dereinst,
Das Schicksal des beneidenswerten Wurms,
Im neuen Sonnental die Flügel rasch
Und freudig zu entfalten!

AUS DEM FÜNFTEN AUFTRITT

Und bin ich denn so elend, wie ich scheine?
Bin ich so schwach, wie ich vor dir mich zeige?
Ist alles denn verloren? Hat der Schmerz,
Als schütterte der Boden, das Gebäude
In einen grausen Haufen Schutt verwandelt?
Ist kein Talent mehr übrig, tausendfältig
Mich zu zerstreun, zu unterstützen? . . .
Nein, alles ist dahin!—Nur eines bleibt:
Die Träne hat uns die Natur verliehen,
Den Schrei des Schmerzens, wenn der Mann zuletzt
Es nicht mehr trägt—Und mir noch über alles—
Sie liess im Schmerz mir Melodie und Rede,
Die tiefste Fülle meiner Not zu klagen:
Und wenn der Mensch in seiner Qual verstummt,
Gab mir ein Gott, zu sagen, wie ich leide.

TORQUATO TASSO ACT V

FROM SCENE 2

If I may not reflect and fashion poems,
then is my life no longer life to me.
As soon forbid the silkworm to spin on
when he is spinning himself close to death!
The precious substance he develops freely
out of his inmost parts and does not cease
till he has sealed himself into his coffin.
That a good god might give us, too, in future
the sweet fate of the enviable worm,
that in a sun-drenched valley we might swiftly
unfold delighted wings.

FROM SCENE 5

Am I indeed as wretched as I seem?
Am I as weak as I have shown myself?
Has everything been lost? Has suffering,
as if the ground had quaked, changed the great castle
into a gruesome pile of burnt-out rubble?
Is there no talent left that thousandfold
could entertain me or support? . . .
No, everything is gone!—One thing remains:
the tear that nature has bestowed on us,
the scream of pain when man can in the end
no longer bear it—and to me yet more—
in pain she left me melody and speech
to mourn the deepest fullness of my grief:
And when man in his agony grows mute,
a god gave me to utter what I suffer.

AUS "VENEZIANISCHE EPIGRAMME"

1

Wie sie klingeln, die Pfaffen! Wie angelegen sie's machen,
Dass man komme, nur ja plappre, wie gestern so heut!
Scheltet mir nicht die Pfaffen; sie kennen des Menchen Bedürfnis!
Denn wie ist er beglückt, plappert er morgen wie heut!

2

„Warum willst du den Christen des Glaubens selige Wonne
Grausam rauben?" Nicht ich, niemand vermag es zu tun.
Steht doch deutlich geschrieben: die Heiden toben vergeblich.
Seht, ich erfülle die Schrift, lest und erbaut euch an mir.

3

Juden und Heiden hinaus! so duldet der christliche Schwärmer.
Christ und Heide verflucht! murmelt ein jüdischer Bart.
Mit den Christen an Spies und mit den Juden ins Feuer!
Singet ein türkisches Kind Christen und Juden zum Spott.
Welcher ist der Klügste? Entscheide! Aber sind diese
Narren in deinem Palast, Gottheit, so geh ich vorbei.

4

Was vom Christentum gilt, gilt von den Stoikern: freien
Menschen geziemet es nicht, Christ oder Stoiker sein.

SEVENTEEN "VENETIAN EPIGRAMS"

1

How they ring their bells, these priests! How pressing they make it
that one should come and prate as one did yesterday, now!
Do not berate the priests; they fathom the needs of men!
For how happy are men, prating tomorrow as now.

2

"Why would you cruelly steal from the Christians the blissful rapture
of their dear faith?" Not I, nobody could do that.
Is it not clearly written? The heathen are raging in vain.
See, I fulfil the Word; read and be edified.

3

Jews and heathen away! is the tolerance of the Christian.
Christian and heathen be damned! murmurs a Jewish beard.
Christians ought to be stabbed, and Jews consigned to the flames!
Thus sings a Turkish child, scorning both Christians and Jews.
Which of these is the wisest? Decide it! But as long as these
fools abound in your palace, Godhead, I pass it by.

4

What applies to the Christians, is also true of the Stoics:
Free human beings could not choose to be Christian or Stoic.

5

Mache der Schwärmer sich Schüler wie Sand am Meere—der Sand ist
Sand; die Perle sei mein, du, o vernünftiger Freund!

6

Schüler macht sich der Schwärmer genug und rühret die Menge,
Wenn der vernünftige Mann einzelne Liebende zählt.
Wundertätige Bilder sind meist nur schlechte Gemälde:
Werke des Geist's und der Kunst sind für den Pöbel nicht da.

7

Zürnet nicht, ihr Frauen, dass wir das Mädchen bewundern:
Ihr geniesset des Nachts, was sie am Abend erregt.

8

Jeglichen Schwärmer schlagt mir an Kreuz im dreissigsten Jahre;
Kennt er nur einmal die Welt, wird der Betrogne der Schelm.

9

Dich betriegt der Staatsmann, der Pfaffe, der Lehrer der Sitten,
Und dies Kleeblatt, wie tief betest du Pöbel es an.
Leider lässt sich noch kaum was rechtes denken und sagen,
Das nicht grimmig den Staat, Götter und Sitten verletzt.

5

Though the enthusiast have pupils like sand at the sea—the sand is
sand; let the pearl be mine, O my rational friend.

6

More than enough disciples gains the enthusiast and moves
crowds. But the rational man finds only few that love him.
Miracle-working pictures are mostly wretched paintings:
works of the spirit and art do not exist for the mob.

7

Do not be angry, women, when we admire a girl:
what in the evening she stirs, you will enjoy at night.

8

Every enthusiast nail to the cross in his thirtieth year!
Once they see through the world, those taken in become knaves.

9

You are deceived by statesmen, priests and the teachers of morals;
and this cloverleaf, mob, how you like to adore it!
Even today there's, alas, little worth thinking and saying
that does not grievously flout mores, the state, and the gods.

10

Alle Weiber sind Waare, mehr oder weniger kostet
Sie den begierigen Mann, der sich zum Handel entschliesst.
Glücklich ist die Beständige, die den Beständigen findet,
Einmal nur sich verkauft und auch nur einmal gekauft wird.

11

Das Gemeine lockt jeden; siehst du in Kürze von vielen
Etwas geschehen, sogleich denke nur: „Dies ist gemein."

12

Vieles kann ich ertragen. Die meisten beschwerlichen Dinge
Duld' ich mit ruhigem Mut, wie es ein Gott mir gebeut.
Wenige sind mir jedoch wie Gift und Schlange zuwider,
Viere: Rauch des Tabaks, Wanzen und Knoblauch und †.

13

Wundern kann es mich nicht, dass unser Herr Christus mit Dirnen
Gern und mit Sündern gelebt, geht's mir doch eben auch so.

14

Wundern kann es mich nicht, dass Menschen die Hunde so lieben:
Denn ein erbärmlicher Schuft ist, wie der Mensch, so der Hund.

10

Women are all of them chattels; more or less is the price
for the desirous man who is resolved to purchase.
Happy is she that is constant and finds one equally constant,
selling herself only once, purchased once only, too.

11

What is common lures all; if you should find soon that many
take the same line, at once pause and reflect: "This is common!"

12

Much there is I can stand, and most things not easy to suffer
I bear with quiet resolve, just as a god commands it.
Only a few I find as repugnant as snakes and poison—
these four: tobacco smoke, bedbugs, garlic, and cross.

13

I cannot be surprised that Christ, our Lord, liked to be with
harlots and people who sinned; that is the case with me, too.

14

I cannot be surprised that men should dote so on dogs:
for a contemptible wretch man is as well as the dog.

15

„Wagst du deutsch zu schreiben unziemliche Sachen?"
Mein Guter,
Deutsch dem kleinen Bezirk leider ist griechisch der Welt.

16

Gib mir statt „Der Sch. . . ." ein ander Wort, o Priapus,
Denn ich Deutscher, ich bin übel als Dichter geplagt.
Griechisch nenn ich dich φαλλος, *das klänge doch prächtig den Ohren,*
Und lateinisch ist auch mentula leidlich ein Wort.
Mentula käme von mens, der Sch. . . . ist etwas von hinten,
Und nach hinten war mir niemals ein froher Genuss.

17

Ist es dir Ernst, so zaudre nun länger nicht; mache mich glücklich!
Wolltest du scherzen? es sei, Liebchen, des Scherzes genug!

NÄHE DES GELIEBTEN

Ich denke dein, wenn mir der Sonne Schimmer
Vom Meere strahlt;
Ich denke dein, wenn sich des Mondes Flimmer
In Quellen malt.

15

"You dare to write indecent matters in German?" Dear fellow,
what appears plain to the few, is, alas, Greek to the world.

16

Give me in place of *der Schwanz* another word, O Priapus;
for as a German I have problems enough as a poet.
Greek I could call you *phallos,* which would sound noble and splendid;
and in Latin there is *mentula,* still a good word:
Mentula comes from *mens,* while *der Schwanz* is something behind,
and behind was for me never a real delight.

17

If you are serious, don't hesitate longer but make me happy!
If you were joking, the time, love, for joking is passed.

NEARNESS OF HER LOVER

I think of you when the sun's glorious shimmer
shines from the sea;
I think of you when the moon's pallid glimmer
edges the tree.

Ich sehe dich wenn auf dem fernen Wege
Der Staub sich hebt;
In tiefer Nacht, wenn auf dem schmalen Stege
Der Wandrer bebt.

Ich höre dich, wenn dort mit dumpfem Rauschen
Die Welle steigt;
Im stillen Haine geh ich oft zu lauschen,
Wenn alles schweigt.

Ich bin bei dir, du seist auch noch so ferne,
Du bist mir nah!
Die Sonne sinkt, bald leuchten mir die Sterne.
O wärst du da!

URWORTE. ORPHISCH

ΔΑΙΜΩΝ

Wie an dem Tag, der dich der Welt verliehen,
Die Sonne stand zum Grusse der Planeten,
Bist alsobald und fort und fort gediehen
Nach dem Gesetz, wonach du angetreten.
So musst du sein, dir kannst du nicht entfliehen,
So sagten schon Sibyllen, so Propheten;
Und keine Zeit und keine Macht zerstückelt
Geprägte Form, die lebend sich entwickelt.

I behold you when on the distant ridge
    the dust throws veils,
in deepest night when on the narrow bridge
    the wanderer quails.

I hear your voice when roaring billows glisten
    in thunderous riot.
In the still grove I often walk to listen
    when all is quiet.

I am with you, however far you are,
    I feel you near.
The sun goes down, soon comes the evening star.
    That you were here!

PRIMEVAL WORDS: ORPHIC

DAIMON

As on the day that gave you to the earth
the sun responded to the planets' spinning,
you have been growing ever since your birth
after the law that governed your beginning.
You cannot flee yourself or change your worth,
thus Sybils have and Prophets long been dinning;
no lapse of time nor any force dissolves
a form, once stamped, that through its life evolves.

SELIGE SEHNSUCHT

Sagt es niemand, nur den Weisen,
Weil die Menge gleich verhöhnet:
Das Lebend'ge will ich preisen
Das nach Flammentod sich sehnet.

In der Liebesnächte Kühlung,
Die dich zeugte wo du zeugtest,
Überfällt dich fremde Fühlung
Wenn die stille Kerze leuchtet.

Nicht mehr bleibest du umfangen
In der Finsternis Beschattung,
Und dicht reisset neu Verlangen
Auf zu höherer Begattung.

Keine Ferne macht dich schwierig,
Kommst geflogen und gebannt,
Und zuletzt, des Lichts begierig,
Bist du Schmetterling verbrannt.

Und so lang du das nicht hast,
Dieses: Stirb und werde!
Bist du nur ein trüber Gast
Auf der dunklen Erde.

BLESSED YEARNING

Tell it none except the wise,
for the common crowd defames:
of the living I shall praise
that which longs for death in flames.

In the love night which created
you where you create, a yearning
wakes: you see, intoxicated,
far away a candle burning.

Darkness now no longer snares you,
shadows lose their ancient force,
as a new desire tears you
up to higher intercourse.

Now no distance checks your flight,
charmed you come and you draw nigh
till, with longing for the light,
you are burnt, O butterfly.

And until you have possessed
dying and rebirth,
you are but a sullen guest
on the gloomy earth.

FRIEDRICH VON SCHILLER

(1759-1805)

During the nineteenth century, and even early in the twentieth century, Schiller was widely considered the greatest German poet next to Goethe, and the two names were coupled constantly. This popular estimate was abetted by Goethe's close friendship with Schiller and by Goethe's high esteem of his friend's work; less by the impassioned admiration of Hölderlin who had found inspiration in Schiller's verse. But few German poets since Hölderlin and Goethe have thought so highly of Schiller, and many have disparaged him. The young Nietzsche still accepted the high estimation of Schiller on which he had been brought up; but in his late works he articulated what other German poets have felt, too. In a bitter passage in *The Wagner Case* (1888), he contrasted the two giants of Weimar:

"One knows Goethe's fate in moraline-sour, old-maidish Germany. He always seemed offensive to Germans; he had honest admirers only among Jewesses. Schiller, the 'noble' Schiller, who lambasted their ears with big words—*he* was after their hearts. What did they hold against Goethe? The 'mount of Venus'; and that he had written *Venetian Epigrams*." Later the same year, in *Twilight of the Idols,* Nietzsche included Schiller in a list of "impossible" people, along with Rousseau, Kant, Victor Hugo, Carlyle, and others: "Schiller: or the Moral-Trumpeter of Säckingen."

Most of the poets included in the present volume were also put off by Schiller's excessive moral preaching; and probably all would have agreed that as a poet he is not in the same class with Goethe.

Schiller's ballads, which are long and didactic, do not stand up very well under the strain of being taught, and sometimes learned by heart, in the secondary schools of Germany; but his epigrammatic distichs are occasionally scarcely distinguishable from Goethe's. For some time, the two poets published their so-called *Xenien* together, unsigned.

Schiller made his living as a professor of history and wrote, for example, a study of the Thirty Years War. He made his reputation not only by his poems but, at least as much, as a dramatist; especially with *Wallenstein* (1798–99) and *Tell* (1804). Since the Nazi era, his once tedious "nobility" may strike some readers as refreshingly clean; his solid decency, as rare and exquisite.

Among Schiller's greatest admirers was Dostoevsky, and George Steiner has shown in *Tolstoy or Dostoevsky* (1959) how the latter's tale of "The Grand Inquisitor," in *The Brothers Karamazov,* contains some echoes of Schiller's play, *Don Carlos* (1787).

Schiller's long poem on "The Gods of Greece" (1788) is discussed briefly in the preface to Heine, below.

ARCHIMEDES UND DER SCHÜLER

Zu Archimedes kam ein wissbegieriger Jüngling.
„Weihe mich“, sprach er zu ihm, „ein in die göttliche Kunst,
Die so herrliche Frucht dem Vaterlande getragen
Und die Mauern der Stadt vor der Sambuca beschützt!“
„Göttlich nennst du die Kunst? Sie ist's“, versetzte der Weise,
„Aber das war sie, mein Sohn, eh' sie dem Staat noch gedient.
Willst du nur Früchte von ihr, die kann auch die Sterbliche zeugen;
Wer um die Göttin freit, suche in ihr nicht das Weib.“

KANT UND SEINE AUSLEGER

Wie doch ein einziger Reicher so viele Bettler in Nahrung
Setzt! Wenn die Könige baun, haben die Kärrner zu tun.

DAS PHILOSOPHISCHE GESPRÄCH

Einer, das höret man wohl, spricht nach *dem andern, doch keiner*
Mit *dem andern; wer nennt zwei Monologen Gespräch?*

ARCHIMEDES AND THE STUDENT

To Archimedes said a youth who desired knowledge:
"Could you initiate me into the art divine
that has engendered such glorious fruit for the fatherland
by protecting our walls from Marcellus' *Sambuca*?"
"Divine you consider this art? Indeed, it is," said the sage;
"but so it was, my dear boy, when it had not served the state.
If you want only the fruit, that can be had, too, from mortals;
but if the goddess you woo, don't seek the female in her."

KANT AND HIS INTERPRETERS

One who is opulent offers legions of famishing beggars
food. When the kings construct, carters find plenty of work.

PHILOSOPHICAL CONVERSATION

After each other they speak, but neither speaks with the other.
Monologues we hear two, dialogue none at all.

DAS DEUTSCHE REICH

Deutschland? aber wo liegt es? Ich weiss das Land nicht zu finden.
Wo das gelehrte beginnt, hört das politische auf.

DEUTSCHER NATIONALCHARAKTER

Zur Nation *euch zu bilden, ihr hoffet es, Deutsche, vergebens;*
Bildet, ihr könnt es, dafür freier zu Menschen euch aus.

DAS HÖCHSTE

Suchst du das Höchste, das Grösste? Die Pflanze kann es dich lehren.
Was sie willenlos ist, sei du es wollend—das ist's!

UNSTERBLICHKEIT

Vor dem Tod erschrickst du? Du wünschest, unsterblich zu leben?
Leb' im Ganzen! Wenn du lange dahin bist, es bleibt.

DEUTSCHES REICH

Germany? But where is it? I cannot find such a country.
Where the culture begins, ends the political realm.

GERMAN NATIONAL CHARACTER

To make yourselves a nation, that you hope vainly, O Germans.
Rather remake yourselves doubly free and humane.

THE HIGHEST

That which is highest and greatest you seek? The plant can instruct you:
What it is without aim, you should be with a will.

IMMORTALITY

You are frightened of death? You wish you could live forever?
Make your life whole! When death takes you that will remain.

UNTERSCHIED DER STÄNDE

Adel ist auch in der sittlichen Welt. Gemeine Naturen
Zahlen mit dem, was sie tun, *edle mit dem, was sie* sind.

JETZIGE GENERATION

War es immer wie jetzt? Ich kann das Geschlecht nicht begreifen:
Nur das Alter ist jung, ach! und die Jugend ist alt.

AUFGABE

Keiner sei gleich dem andern, doch gleich sei jeder dem Höchsten!
Wie das zu machen? Es sei jeder vollendet in sich.

DER SCHLÜSSEL

Willst du dich selber erkennen, so sieh, wie die andern es treiben;
Willst du die andern verstehn, blick in dein eigenes Herz.

CLASS DISTINCTION

In the moral world, too, there's nobility. Common natures
pay with that which they do, noble ones with what they are.

THE NEW GENERATION

Was it always as now? I find this a strange generation:
Only the old appear young; those who are young appear old.

TASK

None should equal the other, but each should equal the highest!
How is this to be done? Each should perfect himself.

THE KEY

If you would know yourself, regard what others are doing;
but if you would understand others consider yourself

POLITISCHE LEHRE

Alles sei recht, was du tust; doch dabei lass es bewenden,
Freund, und enthalte dich ja, alles, was recht ist, zu tun.
Wahrem Eifer genügt, dass das Vorhandne vollkommen
Sei; der Falsche will stets, dass das Vollkommene sei.

MEIN GLAUBE

Welche Religion ich bekenne? Keine von allen,
Die du mir nennst!—Und warum keine?—Aus Religion.

DIE SCHWERE VERBINDUNG

Warum will sich Geschmack und Genie so selten vereinen?
Jener fürchtet die Kraft, dieses verachtet den Zaum.

DER MEISTER

Jeden anderen Meister erkennt man an dem, was er ausspricht;
Was er weise verschweigt, zeigt mir den Meister des Stils.

POLITICAL DOCTRINE

All that you do should be right, but that ought to be sufficient,
friend, and you should not try doing all that is right.
True zeal is satisfied when the existing has been perfected;
misguided zeal always wants that the perfect exist.

MY FAITH

Which religion do I profess? Not one of the many
that you enumerate. Why? Simply out of religion.

THE DIFFICULT COMBINATION

Why is good taste so rarely encountered together with genius?
Taste is afraid of force; genius despises the bridle.

THE MASTER

Masters are known in all other fields by what they express;
that which he wisely says not, shows me the master of style.

DER ABEND

Senke, strahlender Gott—die Fluren dürsten
Nach erquickendem Tau, der Mensch verschmachtet,
Matter ziehen die Rosse—
Senke den Wagen hinab!

Siehe, wer aus des Meers kristallner Woge
Lieblich lächelnd dir winkt! Erkennt dein Herz sie?
Rascher fliegen die Rosse,
Tethys, die göttliche, winkt.

Schnell vom Wagen herab in ihre Arme
Springt der Führer, den Zaum ergreift Cupido,
Stille halten die Rosse,
Trinken die kühlende Flut.

An dem Himmel herauf mit leisen Schritten
Kommt die duftende Nacht; ihr folgt die süsse
Liebe. Ruhet und liebet!
Phöbus, der liebende, ruht.

EVENING

Lower, radiant god—the leas are thirsting
for the refreshing dew, and man is languishing,
wearier walk the horses—
lower the heavenly carriage.

See who is waving at you with a lovely smile
out of the ocean's crystal billow! You know her?
Faster the horses are flying.
Tethys, the goddess, is waving.

Quickly out of the carriage into her arms
leaps the leader while Cupid takes hold of the reins.
Quietly stand the horses,
drinking the cooling water.

Slowly ascending the heavens with measured strides,
fragrant night is coming; the sweetness of love
follows. Rest now and love!
Phoebus, the loving one, rests.

FRIEDRICH HÖLDERLIN

(1770-1843)

Hölderlin vastly admired Goethe and Schiller. Goethe quite failed to recognize his genius; Schiller was kind to him for a while. But as E. M. Butler says in her fascinating book on *The Tyranny of Greece Over Germany* (1935), he is "to all intents and purposes a discovery of the twentieth century, with the notable exception of Nietzsche who knew and revered him" (p. 238). Now he is widely considered Germany's greatest poet after Goethe.

Martin Heidegger has written a whole volume of interpretations of Hölderlin's later, very long poems (*Erläuterungen zu Hölderlins Dichtung*, 1944; rev. ed., with additional chapter, 1951); but Hölderlin scholars deny the soundness of his exegeses.

As a student, Hölderlin was a close friend of Hegel, who was born the same year; but by the time Hegel achieved fame, Hölderlin had become hopelessly insane. While making his living as a private tutor, he developed schizophrenia, desperately fought his depressions, spent a short while in an institution, continued to write some of his best verse as late as 1802 and even 1803, but rapidly became a complete imbecile. In 1807 he was moved into a carpenter's house where he vegetated until his death in 1843.

The first collection of his verse appeared in 1826, edited by Uhland (represented in this volume) and Schwab (remembered chiefly for his collection of the lore of ancient Greece). No single poem can give any adequate idea of the meaning of Greece for Hölderlin, or of the meaning of Hölderlin for growing numbers of German readers. His sense of tragic alienation from the modern world, his despair, too magnificent ever to melt into mere self-pity, and his visions and powerful rhythms have won him not only admiration but love as well.

He wrote a novel in the form of letters, influenced by Goethe's *Werther: Hyperion or the Hermit in Greece* (1797–99). In 1794, Schiller published the first *Fragment* of this work in his periodical, *Thalia.* A drama, *Empedocles,* remained unfinished. Two translations of Sophocles (*Oedipus Rex* and *Antigone*) appeared in 1804.

MENSCHENBEIFALL

Ist nicht heilig mein Herz, schöneren Lebens voll,
Seit ich liebe? warum achtetet ihr mich mehr,
Da ich stolzer und wilder,
Wortereicher und leerer war?

Ach! der Menge gefällt, was auf den Markplatz taugt,
Und es ehret der Knecht nur den Gewaltsamen;
An das Göttliche glauben
Die allein, die es selber sind.

AN DIE PARZEN

Nur einen Sommer gönnt, ihr Gewaltigen!
  Und einen Herbst, zu reifem Gesange mir,
    Dass williger mein Herz, vom süssen
      Spiele gesättiget, dann mir sterbe.

Die Seele, der im Leben ihr göttlich Recht
  Nicht ward, sie ruht auch drunten im Orkus nicht;
    Doch ist mir einst das Heil'ge, das am
      Herzen mir liegt, das Gedicht, gelungen:

Willkommen dann, o Stille der Schattenwelt!
  Zufrieden bin ich, wenn auch mein Saitenspiel
    Mich nicht hinabgeleitet; einmal
      Lebt' ich, wie Götter, und mehr bedarf's nicht.

MEN'S APPLAUSE

Is not holy my heart, full of fairer life
since I love? Why did you respect me more
when I was prouder and wilder,
richer in words and emptier?

Ah, the many admire what is fit for the market!
And the servant will honor only the violent;
in the divine believe
those alone who themselves are divine.

TO THE PARCAE

A single summer grant me, great powers, and
  a single autumn for fully ripened song
    that, sated with the sweetness of my
      playing, my heart may more willingly die.

The soul that, living, did not attain its divine
  right cannot repose in the nether world.
    But once what I am bent on, what is
      holy, my poetry, is accomplished:

Be welcome then, stillness of the shadows' world!
  I shall be satisfied though my lyre will not
      accompany me down there. Once I
        lived like the gods, and more is not needed.

HÄLFTE DES LEBENS

Mit gelben Birnen hänget
Unde voll mit wilden Rosen
Das Land in den See,
Ihr holden Schwäne,
Und trunken von Küssen
Tunkt ihr das Haupt
Ins heilignüchterne Wasser.

Weh mir, wo nehm' ich, wenn
Es Winter ist, die Blumen, und wo
Den Sonnenschein
Und Schatten der Erde?
Die Mauern stehn
Sprachlos und kalt, im Winde
Klirren die Fahnen.

HALF OF LIFE

With yellow pears is hanging
and full of wild-grown roses
the land in the lake:
You lovely swans–
and drunken with kisses
you plunge your head
into sacred sobering water.

Woe's me, where shall I find
when winter comes the flowers and where
the sunny light
and shade of the earth?
The walls will stand
speechless and cold, and pennons
rasp in the wind.

NOVALIS

(1772-1801)

◇◇

Friedrich von Hardenberg, probably the greatest of the early romantic poets, called himself Novalis. In 1794 he met Sophie von Kühn; they became engaged; but in 1797 she died at the age of fifteen. That he sang himself to death with his "Hymns to the Night"—aided by consumption—is better known than the fact that within a year of his fiancée's death he became engaged to another girl whom he desired to keep him company in this world until he succeeded in becoming reunited with his true love, after death.

The text of the "Hymns" here used is that of the original printed version, which appeared in *Athenäum,* a romantic periodical, in 1800. Except for the rhymed portions, the hymns were printed as prose. Later a manuscript version was discovered in which all of the text is written as free verse, and there are also some slight textual differences. Many printed versions follow the manuscript, on the assumption that this must correspond with the poet's intentions, while the *Athenäum* version could have been changed by the editor. But it is, of course, entirely possible that the manuscript represents an earlier draft; and many scholars have argued—convincingly, I think—that the text printed during the poet's lifetime is most likely to reflect his intentions. Moreover, his letters contain no word of disappointment or protest in connection with the printed version.

The "Hymns to the Night" represent the high point of early German romanticism and cast an interesting light on one of the last great achievements of this movement: Richard Wagner's "Liebestod" in *Tristan und Isolde.* The celebration of night and sleep, of the descent below consciousness and the element of pain in ecstasy, had never before found such intense and concentrated form.

Novalis also wrote a novel, *Heinrich von Ofterdingen,* in a deliberate effort to vie with Goethe's *Wilhelm Meister;* an essay, *Die Christenheit oder Europa* (Christendom or Europe); and a large number of philosophical aphorisms. Theodor Haering has devoted a 648-page study to *Novalis als Philosoph* (Novalis as a Philosopher).

HYMNEN AN DIE NACHT: 2

Muss immer der Morgen wiederkommen? Endet nie des Irdischen Gewalt? unselige Geschäftigkeit verzehrt den himmlischen Anflug der Nacht. Wird nie der Liebe geheimes Opfer ewig brennen? Zugemessen ward dem Lichte seine Zeit; aber zeitlos und raumlos ist der Nacht Herrschaft.–Ewig ist die Dauer des Schlafs. Heiliger Schlaf–beglücke zu selten nicht der Nacht Geweihte in diesem irdischen Tagewerk. Nur die Toren verkennen dich und wissen von keinem Schlafe, als dem Schatten, den du in jener Dämmerung der wahrhaften Nacht mitleidig auf uns wirfst. Sie fühlen dich nicht in der goldnen Flut der Trauben–in des Mandelbaums Wunderöl, und dem braunen Safte des Mohns. Sie wissen nicht, dass du es bist, der des zarten Mädchens Busen umschwebt und zum Himmel den Schoss macht–ahnden nicht, dass aus alten Geschichten du himmelöffnend entgegentrittst und den Schlüssel trägst zu den Wohnungen der Seligen, unendlicher Geheimnisse schweigender Bote.

THE SECOND OF THE HYMNS TO THE NIGHT

Must morning always come again? Does the power of earthly things never end? Unblessed busy-ness consumes the heavenly advent of night. Will love's secret sacrifice never burn eternally? To light its time has been measured; but timeless and spaceless is the dominion of night. —Eternally endures sleep. Holy sleep! do not bring joy too rarely to those who in earth's daily labor are dedicated to night. Only the fools mistake you and know of no sleep but that shadow which in the twilight of genuine night you cast over us in compassion. They do not feel you in the golden flood of the grapes, in the miraculous oil of the almond tree, and the brown juice of the poppy. They do not know that it is you that hovers around the tender girl's bosom and makes the womb heaven; do not suspect that from ancient stories you confront us, opening heaven, carrying the key to the abodes of the blessed, of infinite mysteries the silent messenger.

AUS DER VIERTEN HYMNE AN DIE NACHT

Hinüber wall ich,
Und jede Pein
Wird einst ein Stachel
Der Wollust sein.
Noch wenig Zeiten,
So bin ich los,
Und liege trunken
Der Lieb im Schoss.
Unendliches Leben
Wogt mächtig in mir
Ich schaue von oben
Herunter nach dir.
An jenem Hügel
Verlischt dein Glanz—
Ein Schatten bringet
Den kühlenden Kranz.
O! sauge, Geliebter,
Gewaltig mich an,
Dass ich entschlummern
Und lieben kann.
Ich fühle des Todes
Verjüngende Flut,
Zu Balsam und Äther
Verwandelt mein Blut—
Ich lebe bei Tage
Voll Glauben und Mut
Und sterbe die Nächte
In heiliger Glut.

THE RHYMED PART OF THE FOURTH HYMN TO THE NIGHT

Beyond I wander,
all pain will be
ere long a spur
of ecstasy.
A short span of time,
I'm free and above,
and drunken I lie
in the lap of love.
Infinite life
surges in me with might;
and down toward you
I incline my sight.
Your splendor is dying
on yonder hill.
A shadow brings
the wreath of chill.
Suck me toward you, beloved,
with all your force
that I may slumber
and love at last.
I am touched by death's
youth-giving flood,
to balsam and ether
is turned my blood.
I live by day
full of courage and trust,
and die every night
in holy lust.

JOSEPH VON EICHENDORFF

(1788-1857)

A friend of such romantics as Arnim and Brentano, Eichendorff is probably the greatest of the later romantic poets. He fought in the "Wars of Liberation" against Napoleon, then became a civil servant. His pure and beautiful lyrical poems have won wide popularity, but his range was limited. One might almost say that he wrote the same innocuous poem over and over again; and that other romantics, such as Annette von Droste-Hülshoff (1797–1848), Germany's most renowned woman poet, joined him in varying pretty much the same poem—the one that follows. Incidentally, both of them, and Novalis as well, were born into noble families, and not knighted for their accomplishments like Goethe and Schiller.

Among his prose creations, the little novella, *Aus dem Leben eines Taugenichts* (1826, From the Life of a Good-for-Nothing) is outstanding. Of the later poets represented in this volume, Herman Hesse shows the greatest kinship with Eichendorff; especially the early Hesse. But Hesse owes his rank to his later novels, written after World War I; and these are much more complex and richer than his pure and sensitive *juvenilia.*

DER EINSIEDLER

Komm, Trost der Welt, du stille Nacht!
Wie steigst du von den Bergen sacht,
Die Lüfte alle schlafen,
Ein Schiffer nur noch, wandermüd,
Singt übers Meer sein Abendlied
Zu Gottes Lob im Hafen.

Die Jahre wie die Wolken gehn
Und lassen mich hier einsam stehn,
Die Welt hat mich vergessen,
Da tratst du wunderbar zu mir,
Wenn ich beim Waldesrauschen hier
Gedankenvoll gesessen.

O Trost der Welt, du stille Nacht!
Der Tag hat mich so müd gemacht,
Das weite Meer schon dunkelt,
Lass ausruhn mich von Lust und Not,
Bis dass das ew'ge Morgenrot
Den stillen Wald durchfunkelt.

THE HERMIT

Come, O world's comfort, silent night!
Rise from the hills, your step so light
air's sleep it does not raise!
Only a sailor who was long
at sea sings a sad evening song
in port to give God praise.

Like clouds, year blows by after year,
leaving me lonely, standing here,
forgotten by the world.
Then, wonderfully, you drew nigh
when near the forest's rustling I
would sit immersed in thought.

O the world's comfort, silent night!
The day has tired me, the wide
sea darkens, light is gone.
Let me have rest from joys and woes
until the silent forest glows
in the eternal dawn.

LUDWIG UHLAND

(1787-1862)

Uhland studied law and became a lawyer, but later, in 1829, he became a professor of German literature at the University of Tübingen. When the government refused him a leave of absence, which he required as a member of the state parliament, he resigned his professorship in 1833. In 1848 he was elected to the National Convention at Frankfurt, as a liberal.

He wrote several plays, but none of them ever approximated the popularity of his many short ballads. "Bertran de Born" is one of his best. It was first printed in 1829. Heine's poem on the same theme, also included in this volume, appeared in 1839 and is plainly based on Uhland's. Both poets idealized the Provençal bard whom Dante had consigned to hell. While Dante had him carry his head under his arm, as a fit punishment for sowing sedition, Uhland and Heine saw in him an image of nobility that prefigures Nietzsche's conception of the *Übermensch* (overman).

BERTRAN DE BORN

Droben auf dem schroffen Steine
Raucht in Trümmern Autafort,
Und der Burgherr steht gefesselt
Vor des Königs Zelte dort:
„Kamst du, der mit Schwert und Liedern
Aufruhr trug von Ort zu Ort,
Der die Kinder aufgewiegelt
Gegen Ihres Vaters Wort?

„Steht vor mir, der sich gerühmet
In vermess'ner Prahlerei,
Dass ihm nie mehr als die Hälfte
Seines Geistes nötig sei?
Nun der halbe dich nicht rettet,
Ruf den ganzen doch herbei,
Dass er neu dein Schloss dir baue,
Deine Ketten brech' entzwei!"—

„Wie du sagst, mein Herr und König,
Steht vor dir Bertran de Born,
Der mit einem Lied entflammte
Perigord und Ventadorn,
Der dem mächtigen Gebieter
Stets im Auge war ein Dorn,
Dem zu Liebe Königskinder
Trugen ihres Vaters Zorn.

BERTRAN DE BORN

High up on the craggy mountain
smokes in ruins Autafort,
and in chains the castle's master
stands before his royal lord:
"Is it you who wrought sedition
everywhere with song and sword,
who incited loyal children
to defy their father's word?

Did the man that here confronts me
boast with infinite conceit
that he never needed more than
half his spirit, half his wit?
Now that half cannot deliver
you, invoke the whole of it
that it may rebuild your castle,
break your chains, and make you quit!"

"As you say, my king and master,
you confront Bertran de Born,
who once with a song incited
Perigord and Ventadorn,
who was in the mighty ruler's
royal flesh a constant thorn,
for whose sake the king's own children
bore their father's wrath and scorn.

„Deine Tochter sass im Saale
Festlich, eines Herzogs Braut,
Und da sang vor ihr mein Bote,
Dem ein Lied ich anvertraut,
Sang, was einst ihr Stolz gewesen,
Ihres Dichters Sehnsuchtlaut,
Bis ihr leuchtend Brautgeschmeide
Ganz von Tränen war betaut.

„Aus des Ölbaums Schlummerschatten
Fuhr dein bester Sohn empor,
Als mit zorn'gen Schlachtgesängen
Ich bestürmen liess sein Ohr;
Schnell war ihm das Ross gegürtet,
Und ich trug das Banner vor,
Jenem Todespfeil entgegen,
Der ihn traf vor Montforts Tor.

„Blutend lag er mir im Arme;
Nicht der scharfe, kalte Stahl,
Dass er sterb' in deinem Fluche,
Das war seines Sterbens Qual.
Strecken wollt' er dir die Rechte
Über Meer, Gebirg und Tal;
Als er deine nicht erreichet,
Drückt' er meine noch einmal.

In a festive hall your daughter
sat and dined, a ducal bride,
when she heard the song that I had
in a messenger confided,
and he sang the poet's longing,
all that once had been her pride,
till her glistening bridal jewels
shone with tears she could not hide.

In the olive's sleepy shadow
your best son could sleep no more
when he heard my messengers
singing angry songs of war.
Quickly his own steed was saddled,
and the banner that I bore
led him to the deadly arrow
at the portal of Montfort.

In my arms he rested bleeding;
not the icy, cutting steel—
that he died cursed by his father
was the pain he had to feel.
How he wished to stretch his right hand
over ocean, hill, and dale;
finding that he could not reach yours,
he pressed mine with dying zeal.

„Da, wie Autafort dort oben,
Ward gebrochen meine Kraft;
Nicht die ganze, nicht die halbe
Blieb mir, Saite nicht, noch Schaft.
Leicht hast du den Arm gebunden,
Seit der Geist mir liegt in Haft;
Nur zu einem Trauerliede
Hat er sich noch aufgerafft."

Und der König senkt die Stirne:
„Meinen Sohn hast du verführt,
Hast der Tochter Herz verzaubert,
Hast auch meines nun gerührt:
Nimm die Hand, du Freund des Toten,
Die, verzeihend, ihm gebührt!
Weg die Fesseln! Deines Geistes
Hab' ich einen Hauch verspürt."

Then, like Autafort, in ruins
on the rock, my strength did fail;
not the whole, nor even half that,
neither sword nor strings stayed hale.
Easily you chained the body
since my spirit dwells in jail;
wit is gone, the only poem
that remains now is to wail."

And the king inclined his forehead:
"My own son you led to death,
charmed the heart of my poor daughter,
now my own heart is unnerved.
Take my hand, friend of my dead son,
and the pardon he deserved!
Off then with the fetters! Of your
spirit I have felt a breath."

HEINRICH HEINE

(1797-1856)

◇◇

In the period from about 1830 until at least 1880, if not 1900, Germany had only one world-historical poet, Heinrich Heine. In the English-speaking world he is chiefly known for his early love songs; and it is often said that he approximated the simplicity of folk songs. During the Nazi period he was proscribed in Germany, because he was a Jew, and his song, "Ich weiss nicht was soll es bedeuten, dass ich so traurig bin" (I do not know what it should mean that I am so sad) was printed in some anthologies with the notation "author unknown."

Much earlier, Stefan George had envisaged Heine as an evil influence; and his most talented and influential disciple, Friedrich Gundolf, himself born a Jew with the name of Gundelfinger, had articulated the master's ideas in his book on *Stefan George* (1920), in the first chapter: "Time and Task." Here Heine is pictured as "the founder of journalism, of day labor. He is as an anticipating master what thousands ever since have been as wretched slaves: a journalist right down into his lyric poetry—while Goethe had been a poet even in his daily labors . . . For the German language he has become the catastrophic figure who has made things easy and mixed and shifted everything. It is only since Heine that everybody can talk about things that lie beyond the sphere of his soul. He has . . . replaced the sense of weight with the sense for 'nuances.' He has made it possible for soda-jerks to resort to the priest's tone, for orators to turn to lyric language, and for bankers to sound unctuous. He enters many different levels at will, and thus destroys every niveau. He has not created a new niveau of language, like Nietzsche who, in spite of his immeasurable diversity of tone, yet has only *one* height and depth (as it were, the figured bass) . . . Heine begins, and this is no small achievement, the anarchy of the German language . . . But above all, he does not have any new idea that belongs to this historic moment; he maintains alongside of each other the neo-paganism of Goethe as an outlook without body or poise, a Protestant Judaism as a pathos without ethos, and the desires of the French Revolution as an aim without faith. Holding these ideas alongside of each other—the very possibility of doing this without fusion—that is what is new about him, that is his seductiveness."

This portrait at the beginning of a book on Stefan George that does not stay this side of idolatry was part of the mythology of the so-called George Circle: The master was to play the Messiah to Nietzsche's John the Baptist, while Heine was the Antichrist who had ushered in that ultimate degradation from which Stefan George would redeem, if not humanity, the German language.

Nietzsche himself, in 1888, had penned a very different view in *Ecce Homo;* but that book was withheld from publication by his sister, and when it first appeared in 1908 (in an expensive limited edition, because the author had written on a manuscript page "For my

Friends"), George had long formed his conception of Nietzsche. Here is Nietzsche's portrait of Heine:

"The highest conception of the lyric poet *Heinrich Heine* gave to me. I seek in vain in all the realms of thousands of years for an equally sweet and passionate music. He possessed that divine malice without which I cannot conceive perfection. I estimate the value of human beings, of races, according to the necessity with which they cannot understand the god apart from the satyr. And how he handles his German! It will be said one day that Heine and I have been by far the first artists of the German language—at an incalculable distance from everything that mere Germans have done with it." (For a discussion of this passage and of Heine's influence on Nietzsche, see my *Nietzsche*, Meridian edition, 323ff.)

Nietzsche's prophecy was fulfilled when Thomas Mann said in "Notiz über Heine" (1908! Note on Heine; reprinted in *Rede und Antwort*, 1922): "Of his works I have long loved the book on Börne most. . . . His psychology of the Nazarene type anticipates Nietzsche. . . . And incidentally this book contains the most magnificent [*genialste*] German prose prior to Nietzsche."

In the singularly unsympathetic and undiscerning Heine chapter of his *Reason and Energy: Studies in German Literature* (1957), Michael Hamburger characterizes the same book as a "vicious attack on Börne" and "an attack on a dead writer that could serve no other purpose than to ease his own emotional stress." Hamburger betters Gundolf's instruction by "attributing genius to Büchner [which is safe enough], while denying it to Heine." But he is quite unaware of Gundolf's and

George's Heine picture and claims specifically that "it was not until 1926 that a highly fastidious and learned man of letters, Rudolf Borchardt, sounded the alarm by explaining why he found it necessary to reduce Heine's poems to 'fragments' in order to include them in his anthology of the best German poetry."

This approach is of a kind with Hamburger's odd claim that by a flippant last line a "whole poem is reduced to the level of a naughty joke." In *The Baths of Lucca,* Chapter IV, Heine offers his own view of the matter: When people reproach him, "You have no sense for pure naturalness; you are a split human being, a split mind," he replies: "Worthy reader, if you want to lament this split, rather lament that the world itself has split right down the center. . . . Whoever boasts of his heart that it has remained whole, only owns that he has a prosaic, remote nook heart. The great world split has gone through mine, and just therefore I know that the great gods have bestowed a great grace upon me above many others and found me worthy of the poet's martyrdom."

Stefan George's and Rudolf Borchardt's convulsive anti-modernity really has something of the air of "remote nooks," while Heine was the herald of Kierkegaard and Dostoevsky, Nietzsche and Gide, Joyce and Mann, Morgenstern, Benn, and Kästner. The poems that follow give no adequate idea of his genius. And Borchardt was quite right that Heine did not write many perfect poems. But instead of celebrating daffodils and nightingales and the nostalgia of evenings, Heine's verse and prose come to grips with the feelings of a sensitive human being in the modern world—more so than any other poet during the preceding hundred years, with only two exceptions, of both of which he himself was aware. One was Byron, the other Goethe; not the Goethe whom the nineteenth century admired, but the Goethe who created Mephistopheles alongside Faust to mock him.

Regarding Heine's prose, Nietzsche's and Thomas Mann's estimates may safely stand. Indeed, no previous German writer equals Heine's perceptiveness and wit or provokes one so often to laugh out loud.

Of the poems that follow, only the first is of the type that has won wide favor in the English-speaking world. The "Songs of Creation" invite comparison with Jean Effel's magnificent series of 84 humorous cartoons, *La création du monde* (1951); and in Section 7 a theme is struck that was later developed by Nietzsche and Thomas Mann. "The Gods of Greece" deliberately uses the title Schiller had given to a long poem of sixteen rhymed stanzas of eight lines each; indeed, Schiller had later published a revised version "For the Friends of the First Edition," and this ran on for twenty-five stanzas. Here is a translation of Schiller's first stanza:

When you ruled over the beauteous world,
and on joy's light line, held in your hand,
blesséd generations were still led,
beauteous beings from a legend land!
When your rapture service still had power,
all was different, all was different far,
when your temples were adorned with flowers,
Venus Amathusia!

Another translation of this stanza, and of two others, as well as a sympathetic discussion of the whole poem and its influence, will be found in E. M. Butler's book, *The Tyranny of Greece over Germany* (Beacon paperback), which contains interesting chapters on Goethe, Schiller, Hölderlin, and Heine, as well as briefer sections on Nietzsche and George.

Heine's "Bertrand de Born" should be compared with Uhland's ballad, translated in full earlier in this volume. "King David" is closer to I Kings 2 than those not familiar with the Bible would expect.

EIN FICHTENBAUM

Ein Fichtenbaum steht einsam
Im Norden auf kahler Höh'.
Ihn schläfert; mit weisser Decke
Umhüllen ihn Eis und Schnee.

Er träumt von einer Palme,
Die fern im Morgenland
Einsam und schweigend trauert
Auf brennender Felsenwand.

UND BIST DU

Und bist du erst mein ehlich Weib,
Dann bist du zu beneiden,
Dann lebst du in lauter Zeitvertreib,
In lauter Plaisir und Freuden.

Und wenn du schiltst, und wenn du tobst,
Ich werd' es geduldig leiden;
Doch wenn du meine Verse nicht lobst,
Lass' ich mich von dir scheiden.

SCHÖPFUNGSLIEDER

1

Im Beginn schuf Gott die Sonne,
Dann die nächtlichen Gestirne;
Hierauf schuf er auch die Ochsen,
Aus dem Schweisse seiner Stirne.

A FIR TREE

A fir tree stands forsaken
far north on a desolate height.
He drowses, with a blanket
the snow wraps him in white.

He dreams of a distant palm tree
that in a southern land
mourns in forsaken silence
over the burning sand.

AFTER OUR WEDDING DAY

After our wedding day
all will envy you,
for you can loaf and you can play,
with nothing else to do.

And when you scold and when you curse
I shall keep still, of course;
but if you do not praise my verse,
I shall get a divorce.

SONGS OF CREATION

1

At the start, god made the sun,
then the nightly constellations;
after this he made the oxen
from his face's perspiration.

Später schuf er wilde Bestien,
Löwen mit den grimmen Tatzen;
Nach des Löwen Ebenbilde
Schuf er hübsche kleine Katzen.

Zur Bevölkerung der Wildnis
Ward hernach der Mensch erschaffen,
Nach des Menschen holdem Bildnis
Schuf er intressante Affen.

Satan sah dem zu und lachte:
Ei, der Herr kopiert sich selber!
Nach dem Bilde seiner Ochsen
Macht er noch am Ende Kälber!

2

Und der Gott sprach zu dem Teufel:
Ich, der Herr, kopier' mich selber,
Nach der Sonne mach' ich Sterne,
Nach den Ochsen mach' ich Kälber

Nach den Löwen mit den Tatzen
Mach' ich kleine liebe Katzen,
Nach den Menschen mach' ich Affen;
Aber du kannst gar nichts schaffen.

3

Ich hab' mir zu Ruhm und Preis erschaffen
Die Menschen, Löwen, Ochsen, Sonne;
Doch Sterne, Kälber, Katzen, Affen
Erschuf ich zu meiner eigenen Wonne.

Later he made savage beasts,
lions, frightening autocrats;
in the lion's image then
he made pretty little cats.

Then, to make sure of a scrimmage,
he created human shapes;
and in man's attractive image
he made interesting apes.

Satan sneered: "The Good Lord copies
his own work! It makes me laugh!
In the image of his oxen
he will yet create a calf!"

2

And the god said to the Devil:
I, the Lord, ape myself—laugh!
First I make the sun, then stars,
first the oxen, then the calf,

first the lion autocrats,
then the little darling cats,
first man, then a monkey string;
but you cannot make a thing.

3

For my glory I have made the shapes
of humans, lions, oxen, sun;
but stars and calves and cats and apes
I have created just for fun.

4

Kaum hab' ich die Welt zu schaffen begonnen,
In einer Woche war's abgethan.
Doch hatt' ich vorher tief ausgesonnen
Jahrtausendlang den Schöpfungsplan.

Das Schaffen selbst ist eitel Bewegung,
Das stümpert sich leicht in kurzer Frist;
Jedoch der Plan, die Überlegung,
Das zeigt erst, wer ein Künstler ist.

Ich hab' allein dreihundert Jahre
Tagtäglich drüber nachgedacht,
Wie man am besten Doktores Juris
Und gar die kleinen Flöhe macht.

5

Sprach der Herr am sechsten Tage:
Hab' am Ende nun vollgebracht
Diese grosse, schöne, Schöpfung,
Und hab' Alles gut gemacht.

Wie die Sonne rosengoldig
In dem Meere wiederstrahlt!
Wie die Bäume grün und glänzend!
Ist nicht Alles wie gemalt?

Sind nicht weiss wie Alabaster
Dort die Lämmchen auf der Flur?
Ist sie nicht so schön vollendet
Und natürlich, die Natur?

4

Once I commenced the work of creation,
it was done a week after I began.
Yet previous to that came excogitation,
for thousands of years, of the whole plan.

Creating itself is simple motion
and bungled together quickly at will;
the plan, however, the whole notion,
that is what shows the artist's skill.

I worried every single day
for easily three centuries
how to make men with law degrees,
and how to fashion little fleas.

5

Said the Lord on the sixth day:
I have had the hardihood
to complete this great creation;
everything I made is good.

How the sun shines on the sea,
and the sea seems crimson-tainted!
How the trees look green and splendid!
Does it not look as if painted?

Are not white as alabaster
the small lambs there on the pasture?
Is not beautiful and perfect
and quite natural, too, nature?

Erd' und Himmel sind erfüllet
Ganz von meiner Herrlichkeit,
Und der Mensch er wird mich loben
Bis in alle Ewigkeit!

6

Der Stoff, das Material des Gedichts
Das saugt sich nicht aus dem Finger;
Kein Gott erschafft die Welt aus Nichts,
So wenig, wie irdische Singer.

Aus vorgefundenem Urweltsdreck
Erschuf ich die Männerleiber,
Und aus dem Männerrippenspeck
Erschuf ich die schönen Weiber.

Den Himmel erschuf ich aus der Erd'
Und Engel aus Weiberentfaltung;
Der Stoff gewinnt erst seinen Werth
Durch künstlerische Gestaltung.

7

Warum ich eigentlich erschuf
Die Welt, ich will es gern bekennen:
Ich fühlte in der Seele brennen
Wie Flammenwahnsinn den Beruf.

Krankheit ist wohl der letzte Grund
Des ganzen Schöpferdrangs gewesen;
Erschaffend konnte ich genesen,
Erschaffend wurde ich gesund.

Heaven now declares my glory,
earth declares my brilliancy,
and man certainly will praise me
into all eternity!

6

The stuff, the material of poems, you know,
one cannot suck from a finger;
no god makes worlds *ex nihilo,*
any more than an earthly singer.

I made men's bodies from forsaken
primeval filth out of Hades,
and out of men's rib-region bacon
I made the beautiful ladies.

The heaven I made out of the earth,
and angels from women's unfolding;
the matter only wins its worth
by way of artistic molding.

7

The reason for the whole creation
I am quite willing to impart:
I did feel burning in my heart
like flaming madness the vocation.

Disease was the most basic ground
of my creative urge and stress;
creating I could convalesce,
creating I again grew sound.

DIE GÖTTER GRIECHENLANDS

Vollblühender Mond! In deinem Licht,
Wie fliessendes Gold, erglänzt das Meer;
Wie Tagesklarheit, doch dämmrig verzaubert,
Liegt's über der weiten Strandesfläche;
Und am hellblaun, sternlosen Himmel
Schweben die weissen Wolken,
Wie kolossale Götterbilder
Von leuchtendem Marmor.

Nein, nimmermehr, das sind keine Wolken!
Das sind sie selber, die Götter von Hellas,
Die einst so freudig die Welt beherrschten,
Doch jetzt, verdrängt und verstorben,
Als ungeheure Gespenster dahinziehn
Am mitternächtlichen Himmel.

Staunend und seltsam geblendet, betracht' ich
Das luftige Pantheon,
Die feierlich stummen, graunhaft bewegten
Riesengestalten.
Der dort ist Kronion, der Himmelskönig,
Schneeweiss sind die Locken des Haupts,
Die berühmten, Olympos-erschütternden Locken;
Er hält in der Hand den erloschenen Blitz,
In seinem Antlitz liegt Unglück und Gram,
Und doch noch immer der alte Stolz.
Das waren bessere Zeiten, o Zeus,
Als du dich himmlisch ergötztest
An Knaben und Nymphen und Hekatomben!
Doch auch die Götter regieren nicht ewig,

THE GODS OF GREECE

Full flowering moon! In your light,
like flowing gold, the sea is resplendent;
and over the wide expanse of the beach,
daylike clarity touched by the magic of twilight;
and on the light blue, starless sky
white clouds are floating
like colossal statues of gods
made of shining marble.

No, nevermore! Those are no clouds!
These are the gods of Hellas themselves,
that once ruled so gaily over the world,
but now, pushed aside and deceased,
pass along as tremendous specters
on the midnight sky.

Marveling and strangely blinded, I contemplate
the airy pantheon,
the solemnly silent, gruesomely moving
titanic shapes.
That one is Cronion, the king of the heavens;
snow white are the locks on his head,
the famous, Olympos-shattering locks.
In his hand he holds extinguished lightning,
in his countenance lie misfortune and grief,
and yet still the ancient pride.
Those used to be better times, O Zeus,
when you took heavenly pleasure
in boys and in nymphs and in hecatombs!
Yet even the gods do not rule for ever:

Die jungen verdrängen die alten,
Wie du einst selber den greisen Vater
Und deine Titanen-Öhme verdrängt hast,
Jupiter Parricida!
Auch dich erkenn' ich, stolze Juno!
Trotz all deiner eifersüchtigen Angst,
Hat doch eine Andre das Scepter gewonnen,
Und du bist nicht mehr die Himmelskön'gin,
Und dein grosses Aug' ist erstarrt,
Und deine Lilienarme sind kraftlos,
Und nimmermehr trifft deine Rache
Die gottbefruchtete Jungfrau
Und den wundertätigen Gottessohn.
Auch dich erkenn' ich, Pallas Athene!
Mit Schild und Weisheit konntest du nicht
Abwehren das Götterverderben?
Auch dich erkenn' ich, auch dich, Aphrodite,
Einst die goldene! jetzt die silberne!
Zwar schmückt dich noch immer des Gürtels Liebreiz,
Doch graut mir heimlich vor deiner Schönheit,
Und wollt' mich beglücken dein gütiger Leib,
Wie andre Helden, ich stürbe vor Angst—
Als Leichengöttin erscheinst du mir,
Venus Libitina!
Nicht mehr mit Liebe blickt nach dir,
Dort, der schreckliche Ares.
Es schaut so traurig Phöbus Apollo,
Der Jüngling. Es schweigt seine Lei'r,
Die so freudig erklungen beim Göttermahl.
Noch trauriger schaut Hephaistos,
Und wahrlich! der Hinkende, nimmermehr
Fällt er Heben ins Amt,

the young push aside the old,
as you yourself once pushed aside
the ancient father as well as your titan uncles,
Jupiter Parricida!
You, too, I recognize, proud Juno!
Despite all your jealous anxiety,
another woman yet gained the scepter,
and you are no longer the queen of the heavens,
and your great eye has frozen,
and your lily arms are void of strength,
and your revenge will nevermore strike
the god-impregnated virgin
and the miracle-mongering son of the god.
You, too, I recognize, Pallas Athena!
With shield and wisdom you were unable to
fend off the catastrophe of the gods?
You, too, I recognize, you, too, Aphrodite,
golden once, and now silver!
Though the charm of the girdle still adorns you,
I secretly dread your beauty,
and if your gracious body should deign to delight me
like other heroes, I'd die of fright:
as a carcass goddess you appear to me,
Venus Libitina!
It is no longer with love that
the terrible Ares over there looks at you.
So sad looks Phoebus Apollo,
the youth. Silent rests his lyre
that formerly sounded so gay at the feasts of the gods.
Still sadder looks Hephaistos,
and, verily, nevermore will the limper
interfere with the office of Hebe

Und schenkt geschäftig in der Versammlung
Den lieblichen Nektar.—Und längst ist erloschen
Das unauslöschliche Göttergelächter.

Ich hab' euch niemals geliebt, ihr Götter!
Denn widerwärtig sind mir die Griechen,
Und gar die Römer sind mir verhasst.
Doch heil'ges Erbarmen und schauriges Mitleid
Durchströmt mein Herz,
Wenn ich euch jetzt da droben schaue,
Verlassene Götter,
Todte, nachtwandelnde Schatten,
Nebelschwache, die der Wind verscheucht—
Und wenn ich bedenke, wie feig und windig
Die Götter sind, die euch besiegten,
Die neuen, herrschenden, tristen Götter,
Die Schadenfrohen im Schafspelz der Demut—
O, da fasst mich ein düsterer Groll,
Und brechen möcht' ich die neuen Tempel,
Und kämpfen für euch, ihr alten Götter,
Für euch und eu'r gutes ambrosisches Recht,
Und vor euren hohen Altären,
Den wiedergebauten, den opferdampfenden,
Möcht' ich selber knieen und beten,
Und flehend die Arme erheben—

Denn immerhin, ihr alten Götter,
Habt ihr's auch ehmals in Kämpfen der Menschen
Stets mit der Partei der Sieger gehalten,
So ist doch der Mensch grossmüt'ger als ihr,
Und in Götterkämpfen halt' ich es jetzt
Mit der Partei der besiegten Götter.

and busily pour sweet nectar
at their assembly.—And long has been extinguished
the inextinguishable laughter of the gods.

I have never loved you, O gods!
For an abomination to me are the Greeks,
and the Romans are yet more hateful to me.
Yet holy mercy and dreadful pity
flow through my heart
when I now behold you up there,
abandoned gods,
dead, sleepwalking shadows,
weak as a mist that the wind puts to flight—
and when I consider how windy and cowardly
the gods are that vanquished you,
the new, now dominant, dismal gods,
who relish our pains, in meekness' sheep's clothing.
Oh, then a gloomy wrath comes over me,
and I would break the new temples
and fight for you, O you ancient gods,
for you and your good ambrosian right;
and before your lofty altars,
rebuilt and steaming again with sacrifices,
I myself should like to kneel and to pray,
raising up my arms to implore.

For after all, you ancient gods,
even though formerly in the fights between men
you have always been on the side of the winners,
man is certainly more magnanimous than you,
and in the fights between gods I now side
with the vanquished gods.

Also sprach ich, und sichtbar erröteten
Droben die blassen Wolkengestalten,
Und schauten mich an wie Sterbende,
Schmerzenverklärt, und schwanden plötzlich;
Der Mond verbarg sich eben
Hinter Gewölke, das dunkler heranzog;
Hoch aufrauschte das Meer,
Und siegreich traten hervor am Himmel
Die ewigen Sterne.

BERTRAND DE BORN

Ein edler Stolz in allen Zügen,
Auf seiner Stirn Gedankenspur,
Er konnte jedes Herz besiegen,
Bertrand de Born, der Troubadour.

Es kirrten seine süssen Töne
Die Löwin des Plantagenet's;
Die Tochter auch, die beiden Söhne,
Er sang sie Alle in sein Netz.

Wie er den Vater selbst betörte!
In Tränen schmolz des Königs Zorn,
Als er ihn lieblich reden hörte,
Den Troubadour, Bertrand de Born.

Thus I spoke, and above me
the pale shapes of the clouds reddened visibly
and looked at me like those dying,
transfigured by suffering, and suddenly vanished;
the moon concealed herself
behind darker clouds that drew near;
the sea leapt up high,
and in the heavens emerged triumphant
eternal stars.

BERTRAND DE BORN

In every feature noble pride,
upon his brow the print of thought,
there was no heart he could not guide,
Bertrand de Born, the troubadour.

He lured with his enchanting tones
the lioness of Plantagenet,
the daughter also, both the sons—
he sang them all into his net.

How he bewitched the father, too!
In tears melted the royal scorn,
dissolved by dulcet language through
the troubadour, Bertrand de Born.

KÖNIG DAVID

Lächelnd scheidet der Despot,
Denn er weiss, nach seinem Tod
Wechselt Willkür nur die Hände,
Und die Knechtschaft hat kein Ende.

Armes Volk! wie Pferd und Farrn
Bleibt es angeschirrt am Karrn,
Und der Nacken wird gebrochen,
Der sich nicht bequemt den Jochen.

Sterbend spricht zu Salomo
König David: Apropos,
Dass ich Joab dir empfehle.
Einen meiner Generäle.

Dieser tapfre General
Ist seit Jahren mir fatal,
Doch ich wagte den Verhassten
Niemals ernstlich anzutasten.

Du, mein Sohn, bist fromm und klug,
Gottesfürchtig, stark genug,
Und es wird dir leicht gelingen,
Jenen Joab umzubringen.

KING DAVID

Smiling on his death bed lies
the old despot: when he dies,
tyranny will but change hands;
and oppression never ends.

Oxlike, the poor common folk
remain harnessed to the yoke,
and the neck is quickly snapped
that refuses to stay trapped.

David on his dying bed
spoke to Solomon and said,
knowing all this: "Apropos,
there is Joab, as you know.

This courageous general
I no longer like so well,
but for years I dared not touch
him I'd come to hate so much.

You are pious, have the stuff,
are God-fearing, strong enough
to find means without delay
to put him out of the way."

CONRAD FERDINAND MEYER

(1825-1898)

Meyer, a Swiss, was born in, and died near, Zurich. As a young man, he became more and more neurotic, developed delusions, finally suffered a breakdown, and in 1852 consented to being committed to an asylum near Neuchâtel. After seven months he was released, and spent some time in Lausanne before returning home. In 1856 his mother developed an acute melancholia, was taken to the same asylum near Neuchâtel, and soon after drowned herself. Her death seems to have liberated her son. In 1857 he went to Paris for three months, and in 1858 he visited Rome. In 1860 he sent some of his poems to a publisher: "Bilder und Balladen von Ulrich Meister" (Images and Ballads by Ulrich Meister). They were not published. But he continued to work on his verse, and in 1864 his first volume appeared: *Zwanzig Balladen von einem Schweizer* (Twenty Ballads by a Swiss). He was now almost forty. In 1870 he published a second volume of verse, and in 1871 his great cycle of poems, *Huttens letzte Tage* (The Last Days of Hutten).

In 1876 he published his novel, *Jürg Jenatsch,* on which he had been working for ten years. By 1894 it was in its twentieth printing. Of his other, shorter, novels

English-speaking readers may find *Der Heilige* (1880, 12th ed. 1894; The Saint) of special interest because it deals with Thomas à Becket. He completed his last story, *Angela Borgia*, in 1891, and published the final revision of his collected poems in 1892. The same year he suffered a breakdown and, profoundly depressed, returned to the asylum which he had left forty years earlier. After a year he was released and spent the last five years of his life at home.

No German poet of his generation seems to me to approximate Meyer's stature. Among those born during the first half of the nineteenth century, only Nietzsche (born nineteen years later) is of comparable originality and, on account of his prose works, of immensely greater significance. Even if we include the third quarter of the century, only Stefan George is in the same class with Meyer; and it may well be that Meyer was greater. Indeed, it is arguable that the only poet since Meyer's time who has enriched German literature with more great poems, and greater poems, than he did was Rilke.

The second poem offered here, "In the Sistina," reflects Meyer's persistent preoccupation with the Renaissance and with great men; also his recurring attempt to deal with works of art. "The Roman Fountain" (another poem on the same theme by Rilke will be found later in this volume) is a poem Meyer rewrote more than once. An early version of 1866 is still extant, and another one, much closer to the final text, appeared in his collection of 1870. One of Meyer's many ballads rounds out the selection. Perhaps one has to read a lot more of his verse to realize in how many ways Nietzsche, George, and Rilke are close to Meyer.

EINGELEGTE RUDER

Meine eingelegten Ruder triefen.
Tropfen fallen langsam in die Tiefen.

Nichts, das mich verdross! Nichts, das mich freute!
Niederrinnt ein schmerzenloses Heute!

Unter mir—ach, aus dem Licht verschwunden—
Träumen schon die schönern meiner Stunden.

Aus der blauen Tiefe ruft das Gestern:
Sind im Licht noch manche meiner Schwestern?

IN DER SISTINA

In der Sistine dämmerhohem Raum,
Das Bibelbuch in seiner nerv'gen Hand,
Sitzt Michelangelo in wachem Traum,
Umhellt von einer kleinen Ampel Brand.

Laut spricht hinein er in die Mitternacht,
Als lauscht' ein Gast ihm gegenüber hier,
Bald wie mit einer allgewalt'gen Macht,
Bald wieder wie mit seinesgleichen schier:

„Umfasst, umgrenzt hab ich dich, ewig Sein,
Mit meinen grossen Linien fünfmal dort!
Ich hüllte dich in lichte Mäntel ein
Und gab dir Leib, wie dieses Bibelwort.

OARS PULLED UP

Pulled up, resting gently, my oars drip;
slowly drops descend into the deep.

Nothing troubled me, nothing gave joy!
Downward glides a sorrowless today.

Under me, where drops no longer gleam,
fairer hours that have vanished dream.

Yesterday calls from the azure deep:
are yet many sisters not asleep?

IN THE SISTINA

In the Sistina's twilit vaulted land
sits Michelangelo in waking dreams,
a Bible volume in his mighty hand,
and over him a tiny lantern gleams.

He speaks into the middle of the night
as if some guest were listening to his word,
now as if to some superhuman might,
now as if one like him were there and heard.

"Eternal Being, with my sweeping strokes
I bounded and embraced you five times, hid
your glory in five flowing, radiant cloaks,
and gave you body as the Bible did.

Mit wehnden Haaren stürmst du feurigwild
Von Sonnen immer neuen Sonnen zu,
Für deinen Menschen bist in meinem Bild
Entgegenschwebend und barmherzig du!

So schuf ich dich mit meiner nicht'gen Kraft:
Damit ich nicht der grössre Künstler sei,
Schaff mich—ich bin ein Knecht der Leidenschaft—
Nach deinem Bilde schaff mich rein und frei!

Den ersten Menschen formtest du aus Ton,
Ich werde schon von härterm Stoffe sein,
Da, Meister, brauchst du deinen Hammer schon.
Bildhauer Gott, schlag zu! Ich bin der Stein."

DER RÖMISCHE BRUNNEN

Aufsteigt der Strahl und fallend giesst
Er voll der Marmorschale Rund,
Die, sich verschleiernd, überfliesst
In einer zweiten Schale Grund;
Die zweite gibt, sie wird zu reich,
Der dritten wallend ihre Flut,
Und jede nimmt und gibt zugleich
Und strömt und ruht.

With flying hair you storm without restraint
from suns to novel suns with fiery face,
but to the man you fashioned, whom I paint,
you are inclined in flight and show him grace.

Thus I made you although my strength is coarse:
lest I the greater artist be,
make me—I am a slave to passion's force—
in your own image make me, pure and free.

The first man you have shaped from tender clay;
I should be struck out of a harder block:
Your hammer, Master, you will need today.
O sculptor God, strike me: I am the rock."

THE ROMAN FOUNTAIN

Up spurts the beam, falls, and bestows
itself upon the marble round,
which veils itself and overflows
into a second basin's ground;
the second gives, it grows too rich,
the third in waves its falling crest,
and each receives and gives at once,
and streams and rests.

DIE FÜSSE IM FEUER

Wild zuckt der Blitz. In fahlem Lichte steht ein Turm.
Der Donner rollt. Ein Reiter kämpft mit seinem Ross,
Springt ab und pocht ans Tor und lärmt. Sein Mantel saust
Im Wind. Er hält den scheuen Fuchs am Zügel fest.
Ein schmales Gitterfenster schimmert goldenhell
Und knarrend öffnet jetzt das Tor ein Edelmann . . .

—„Ich bin ein Knecht des Königs, als Kurier geschickt
Nach Nîmes. Herbergt mich! Ihr kennt des Königs Rock!"
—„Es stürmt. Mein Gast bist du. Dein Kleid, was kümmert's mich?
Tritt ein und wärme dich! Ich sorge für dein Tier!"
Der Reiter tritt in einen dunkeln Ahnensaal,
Von eines weiten Herdes Feuer schwach erhellt,
Und je nach seines Flackerns launenhaftem Licht
Droht hier ein Hugenott im Harnisch, dort ein Weib,
Ein stolzes Edelweib aus braunem Ahnenbild . . .
Der Reiter wirft sich in den Sessel vor dem Herd
Und starrt in den lebend'gen Brand. Er brütet, gafft . . .
Leis sträubt sich ihm das Haar. Er kennt den Herd, den Saal . . .
Die Flamme zischt. Zwei Füsse zucken in der Glut.

Den Abendtisch bestellt die greise Schaffnerin
Mit Linnen blendend weiss. Das Edelmägdlein hilft.
Ein Knabe trug den Krug mit Wein. Der Kinder Blick
Hangt schreckensstarr am Gast und hangt am Herd entsetzt . . .
Die Flamme zischt. Zwei Füsse zucken in der Glut.

THE FEET IN THE FIRE

Lightning writhes wildly. In the gaunt light a tower.
And thunder rolls. A rider struggles with his horse,
jumps down, knocks at the door, and roars. His cloak blows
in the wind. He holds the shy horse firmly by the reins.
A narrow grated window glistens golden,
and now a nobleman unlocks the creaking gate . . .

"I am a royal knight, sent as a messenger
to Nîmes. Lodge me! You know the royal coat!"
"It storms. You are my guest. Your coat—what's that to me?
Come in and warm yourself! I shall see to your horse!"
The rider steps into a dark ancestral hall,
but weakly lighted by the fire in the hearth,
and, shifting with its moody light,
a well-armed Huguenot threatens here, and there a woman,
proud noblewoman, from a dark brown picture . . .
The rider sinks into an armchair near the hearth
and stares into the living fire. He broods and gapes . . .
His hair is bristling. For he knows the hearth, the hall . . .
The flame is sizzling. Two feet are writhing in the fire.

The aged maid prepares the dinner table
with linen, splendid white. The noble's daughter helps.
A boy carried the pitcher with the wine. The children's glances
are fixed in horror on the guest, and frightened on the hearth . . .
The flame is sizzling. Two feet are writhing in the fire.

–„Verdammt! Dasselbe Wappen! Dieser selbe Saal!
Drei Jahre sinds . . . Auf einer Hugenottenjagd . . .
Ein fein, halsstarrig Weib . . ., Wo steckt der Junker? Sprich!‘
Sie schweigt. ‚Bekenn!‘ Sie schweigt. ‚Gib ihn heraus!‘ Sie schweigt.
Ich werde wild. Der *Stolz! Ich zerre das Geschöpf . . .*
Die nackten Füsse pack ich ihr und strecke sie
Tief mitten in die Glut . . . ‚Gib ihn heraus!‘ . . . Sie schweigt . . .
Sie windet sich . . . Sahst du das Wappen nicht am Tor?
Wer hiess dich hier zu Gaste gehen, dummer Narr?
Hat er nur einen Tropfen Bluts, erwürgt er dich.“–
Eintritt der Edelmann. „Du träumst! Zu Tische, Gast . . .“

Da sitzen sie. Die drei in ihrer schwarzen Tracht
Und er. Doch keins der Kinder spricht das Tischgebet.
Ihn starren sie mit aufgerissnen Augen an–
Den Becher füllt und übergiesst er, stürzt den Trunk,
Springt auf: „Herr, gebet jetzt mir meine Lagerstatt!
Müd bin ich wie ein Hund!“ Ein Diener leuchtet ihm,
Doch auf der Schwelle wirft er einen Blick zurück
Und sieht den Knaben flüstern in des Vaters Ohr . . .
Dem Diener folgt er taumelnd in das Turmgemach.

Fest riegelt er die Tür. Er prüft Pistol und Schwert.
Gell pfeift der Sturm. Die Diele bebt. Die Decke stöhnt.
Die Treppe kracht . . . Dröhnt hier ein Tritt? Schleicht dort ein Schritt? . . .

"Confounded! The same coat of arms! The same hall!
Three years have passed . . . We hunted Huguenots . . .
A fine, stiff-necked woman . . . 'Where is the knight?
Speak up!'
She's silent. 'Confess!' She's silent. 'Give him up!' She's
silent . . .
I become wild. Such pride! I drag the creature . . .
I seize her naked feet and stretch them out
deep, deep into the flames . . . 'Give him up!' She's
silent . . .
She is convulsed . . . Did you not see the coat of arms
above the gate?
Who told you to seek refuge here, you stupid fool?
If he has but a drop of blood, he strangles you."
The nobleman comes in. "You dream! To dinner,
guest . . ."

And there they sit. The three in their black garments,
and he. None of the children say the dinner blessing.
They stare at him with anxious open eyes—
he fills the cup and spills it, gulps his drink,
jumps up: "Sir, show me to my bedroom!
I am tired as a dog!" A servant holds the lantern,
but from the threshold he casts back a glance
and sees the young boy whispering in his father's ear . . .
He reels into the attic room behind the servant.

Firmly he locks the door. He tests pistol and sword.
The storm is howling. The floor trembles. The ceiling
moans.
The stairs are creaking . . . Is that a step? . . . Is
someone creeping? . . .

Ihn täuscht das Ohr. Vorüberwandelt Mitternacht.
Auf seinen Lidern lastet Blei, und schlummernd sinkt
Er auf das Lager. Draussen plätschert Regenflut.
Er träumt. „Gesteh!" Sie schweigt. „Gib ihn heraus!" Sie schweigt.
Er zerrt das Weib. Zwei Füsse zucken in der Glut.
Aufsprüht und zischt ein Feuermeer, das ihn verschlingt . .

—„Erwach! Du solltest längst von hinnen sein! Es tagt!"
Durch die Tapetentür in das Gemach gelangt,
Vor seinem Lager steht des Schlosses Herr—ergraut,
Dem gestern dunkelbraun sich noch gekraust das Haar.

Sie reiten durch den Wald. Kein Lüftchen regt sich heut.
Zersplittert liegen Ästetrümmer quer im Pfad.
Die frühsten Vöglein zwitschern, halb im Traume noch.
Friedsel'ge Wolken schwimmen durch die klare Luft,
Als kehrten Engel heim von einer nächt'gen Wacht.
Die dunkeln Schollen atmen kräft'gen Erdgeruch.
Die Ebne öffnet sich. Im Felde geht ein Pflug.
Der Reiter lauert aus den Augenwinkeln: „Herr,
Ihr seid ein kluger Mann und voll Besonnenheit
Und wisst, dass ich dem grössten König eigen bin.
Lebt wohl! Auf Nimmerwiedersehn!" Der andre spricht:
„Du sagst's! Dem grössten König eigen! Heute ward
Sein Dienst mir schwer... Gemordet hast du teuflisch mir
Mein Weib! Und lebst... Mein ist die Rache, redet Gott."

His ear deceives him. Midnight passes by.
The weight of heavy lead upon his lids, he yields to slumber
on his bed. Outside the rain is splattering.
He dreams. "Confess!" She's silent. "Give him up!" She's silent.
He drags the woman. Two feet are writhing in the fire.
An ocean of flames licks up, sizzles, and swallows him . . .

"Wake up! You should have left here long ago! The dawn is past!"
Entering the room through a wallpapered door,
the castle's lord stands at his bed—turned gray
the hair that was dark brown but yesterday.

They ride through woodland. Not a breeze today.
The broken branches lie in splinters on the path.
The first birds twitter, half immersed in dreams.
Peaceful clouds are swimming through the brilliant air,
as if the angels were returning from their nightly watch.
The dark earth breathes with a healthy smell of soil.
The plain is opening. A plow is moving in the field.
The rider's eyes are sneering: "Sir,
you are a prudent man and circumspect,
and know that I belong to the almighty king.
Farewell. And may I see you nevermore!" The other says:
"You say it! Belong to the Almighty King! Today I found
His service hard . . . You murdered devilishly
my wife and live! . . . Revenge is mine, says God."

FELIX DAHN

(1834-1912)

◇◇

Dahn, who held professorships at Würzburg, Königsberg, and Breslau, is best known for his immensely popular historical novel, *Ein Kampf um Rom* (4 vols. 1876, A Fight for Rome). It deals with the Ostrogoths and their ultimate destruction, and was published during the same year that saw the first performance of Wagner's *Ring* in Bayreuth. Eagerly devoured by generations of schoolboys—on their own, too, not only in class—it did its share to influence conceptions of loyalty and honor. Dahn's plays, including one on Kriemhild's revenge and the destruction of the Burgundians under their king, Gunter, have been generally forgotten; nor was Dahn an important poet. But at least one of his poems, which is well known in Germany from anthologies, is of unusual interest: "Hagen's Dying Song."

Since its significance is hardly due to its poetry, I have given up any attempt to reproduce the rhymes in the middle of the lines. But the translation retains the rhythm and the end rhymes. What is notable is chiefly the glorification of Hagen and the poet's conception of his hero. According to the *Nibelungenlied*, the medieval epic, King Gunter was unable to master his bride, Brunhild, and had to invoke the help of his sister's husband, Siegfried, to subdue the redoubtable Brunhild during his wedding night, so he could consummate his marriage. Later, Brunhild and Kriemhild (Siegfried's wife) meet on the church steps and quarrel. Brunhild taunts Kriemhild by insisting that she is her inferior because Siegfried is Gunter's vassal. Kriemhild, hurt in her pride, tells Brunhild about her wedding night. Brunhild, humiliated beyond endurance, tells Gunter, who summons Siegfried, and both men deny everything. But she also tells Hagen who immediately vows to her that he will save the honor of his king and queen by killing Siegfried. This cannot be done in open combat, as Siegfried is vulnerable only in one small place, between his shoulder blades, where a fallen leaf kept off the dragon's blood in which he bathed his skin to make it forever invulnerable. Therefore, Hagen approaches the hero as he bends down to drink and stabs him in the back.

Kriemhild, resolved to revenge herself, marries Etzel (Attila), the king of the Huns, has him invite her tribe, the Burgundians, and then organizes a slaughter which turns into a terrible battle. In the end, only Gunter and Hagen survive. No Hun can subdue them, but Dietrich von Bern (Theodoric of Verona, the great Gothic king) subdues the two worn-out heroes and delivers them to Kriemhild, bound: Hagen first (the old epic says that "he gave into her hand the boldest hero that ever carried a sword"), then Gunter. Dietrich pleads with her to spare them. Kriemhild taunts them, has them moved to separate dungeons, then confronts Hagen and asks him to return to her the gold of the Nibelungen. Hagen says that he has sworn an oath not to reveal where it is hidden "as long as even one of my lords is alive." Then Kriemhild has her brother's head cut off and carries it by the hair to Hagen, who retorts: "Now it has happened as I had expected. Now the noble king of Burgundy is dead," and so are all the princes; "now nobody knows of the treasure but God and I alone; so it will remain hidden from you for ever." Kriemhild then strikes off Hagen's head; and old Hildebrand, seeing this, kills her in his wrath; and that is the end of the Burgundians.

Hagen's song, as conceived by Dahn, will strike some readers as Nietzschean. In the chapter "On The Thousand and One Goals" in the First Part of *Zarathustra* (1883), Nietzsche contrasts the ethics of four peoples, the Greeks, the Persians, the Jews, and the Germans. I shall quote what he says about the last two:

" 'To honor father and mother and to follow their will to the root of one's soul'—this was the tablet of overcoming that another people hung up over themselves and became powerful and eternal thereby. 'To practice loyalty and, for the sake of loyalty, to risk honor and blood even for evil and dangerous things'—with this teaching another people conquered themselves; and through this self-conquest they became pregnant and heavy with great hopes."

HAGENS STERBELIED

Nun werd' ich sehr alleine!—Die Fürsten liegen tot:—
Wie glänzt im Mondenscheine der Estrich blutig rot!
Die fröhlichen Burgunden, wie sie nun stille sind!
Ich höre, wie aus Wunden das Blut in Tropfen rinnt.
Es steiget aus dem Hause ein Dunst von Blute schwer,
Schon kreischen nach dem Schmause die Geier ringsumher.
Es schläft der König Gunter in fieberwirrem Schlaf,
Seit ihn vom Turm herunter ein spitzer Bolzen traf.
Und Volker liegt erschlagen; der lachte, wie er fiel:
„Nimm all mein Erbe, Hagen, nimm du mein Saitenspiel."
Er trug, vor Heunentücken geschirmt, die Fiedel traut
Auf seinem sichern Rücken, den nie ein Feind geschaut.
Sie scholl wie Nachtigallen, wenn Volker sie gespannt;
Wohl anders wird sie schallen in meiner harten Hand.
Vier Saiten sind zersprungen,—drei haften noch daran!
Ich habe nie gesungen, ich bin kein Fiedelmann.—
Doch treibt mich's, zu versuchen, wie Hagens Weise geht:
Ich denk', ein gutes Fluchen ist auch kein schlecht Gebet!
So sei'n verflucht die Weiber, Weib ist, was falsch und schlecht:
Hier um zwei weisse Leiber verdirbt Burgunds Geschlecht!
Und Fluch dem Wahngetriebe von Sitte, Liebe, Recht:
Erlogen ist die Liebe, und nur der Hass ist echt.
Die Reue ist der Narren! Nur das ist Atmens wert,
Im Tod noch auszuharren beim Groll, beim Stolz, beim Schwert.

HAGEN'S DYING SONG

Now I am growing lonely. The princes are all dead,
and in the moonshine glimmers the hearth in bloody red.
The once so gay Burgundians are still, their revels stop.
I hear how from their bodies the blood runs drop on drop.
Out of the house arises a heavy smell of blood,
and screeching vultures circle impatient for their food.
King Gunter is still sleeping his fever-maddened sleep,
since a well sharpened arrow struck from the tower steep.
And Volker fell with laughter, and thus bade me adieu:
"Take all I leave, dear Hagen, my strings I leave to you."
Secure from Hunnish cunning, he carried without awe
the fiddle on his safe back that no foe ever saw.
Like nightingales it sounded, strummed by the fearless bard;
no doubt, it will sound different in my hand, which is hard.
Three strings remain to play on, the other four are gone;
I am not used to singing, I am no fiddle man.
And yet I feel like trying how Hagen's tune might go:
I think some good sound cursing is a good prayer, too.
Above all, cursed be women; woman is falsity:
here, for two soft white bodies, perishes Burgundy!
And cursed be the illusion of morals, love, and law:
love is a lying fiction, and only hate is true.
Repentance is for idiots. Nothing has worth beside
enduring still when dying with wrath and sword and pride.

Und hätt' ich zu beraten neu meine ganze Bahn,—
Ich liesse meiner Taten nicht e i n e ungetan.
Und käm', der Welt Entzücken, ein zweiter Siegfried her,—
Ich stiess' ihm in den Rücken zum zweitenmal den Speer!
Was reisst ihr, feige Saiten? Versagt ihr solchem Sang?—
Ha, wer mit mächt'gem Schreiten kommt dort den Hof entlang?
Das ist kein Heunenspäher, das dröhnt wie Schicksalsgang,
Und näher, immer näher:—ein Schatte riesenlang.—
Auf, Gunter, jetzt erwache, den Schritt kenn' ich von fern:
Auf, auf!—Der Tod, die Rache und Dietrich kommt von Bern!

If I must reconsider my deeds now, one by one,
I should not leave a single act that I did undone.
And if, the world's enchantment, another Siegfried came,
I'd stab him in the back, too, with the same deadly aim.
You tear, strings? Are you cowards, afraid of such a song?
Hah, who comes down the courtyard, with strides that are so long?
That is no Hunnish lookout, those are the steps of fate—
and nearer, ever nearer—I recognize his gait.
Up, Gunter, now awaken, this is the final turn:
Up, up! Death, the avenger, and Dietrich comes from Bern!

FRIEDRICH NIETZSCHE

(1844-1900)

◇◇

No other philosopher in any land since Kant and Hegel has equaled their many-sided international influence as Nietzsche did. Unlike Kant and Hegel, Nietzsche was also a writer of brilliant prose, and it is doubtful whether he has any equal among Germans in this respect. As he himself noted in *Ecce Homo*, with a characteristic lack of modesty, only Heine is in the same class with him. (The passage is quoted in the preface to Heine, above.)

In the English-speaking world, it has taken a long time for Nietzsche to be taken seriously as a philosopher, and his impact still does not compare with his pervasive influence on German and French letters. His reputation as a poet is all but non-existent in England and in the United States. In Germany, on the other hand, it is a commonplace that he is one of the most important and influential poets since Hölderlin. Poems on him by George and Morgenstern will be found later in this volume; Benn wrote a poem on him, too, as well as a notable essay quoted below in the preface to Benn; and Rilke's relationship to him is analyzed in detail in two chapters (12 and 13) of my *From Shakespeare to Existentialism*.

The first of the poems that follow was written in 1864. The title is taken from The Acts of the Apostles, in the New Testament. Paul says (17.23): "I found an altar with this inscription, TO THE UNKNOWN GOD." In his later works, Nietzsche gave a name to "the unknown God" he served: "Dionysus."

In 1882 Nietzsche published *Die Fröhliche Wissenschaft* (The Gay Science, mistranslated as *The Joyful Wisdom*) with a "Prelude in German Rhymes" that bore a title taken from Goethe: "Scherz, List und Rache" (Fun, Cunning, and Revenge). Five of the poems from this prelude are offered next. Of these, the one called "Ecce Homo" is probably much the best known. The second edition of the same book (1887) featured a whole new chapter of long aphorisms as well as an Appendix: "Lieder des Prinzen Vogelfrei" (Songs of Prince Free-as-a-Bird; the last phrase generally refers to an outlaw whom anyone may shoot at sight). Two poems from this appendix are offered: "To Goethe" and "To the Mistral." The former is a parody on the final chorus of Goethe's *Faust,* which begins, "What is destructible / is but a parable" and ends "The Eternal-Feminine / lures to perfection." Of the mistral dictionaries say that it is "a violent, cold, and dry northerly wind of the Mediterranean provinces of France"; the poem was written November 22, 1884.

Early in January 1889 Nietzsche suffered a complete mental collapse, and his friend Overbeck came from Basel, where Nietzsche had been a professor of classical philology from 1869 until his resignation ten years later, to take Nietzsche back home, to an asylum if necessary. On the train Nietzsche, no longer able to sustain any sensible conversation, stunned Overbeck by reciting a very striking poem. (André Malraux has incorporated this episode in *La lutte avec l'ange.*) Later it turned out to be part of *Ecce Homo*, a book Nietzsche had completed a few months earlier. In the book the poem has no title, but in posthumous editions of Nietzsche's poetry it is generally called "Venice." It is offered here.

"The Sun Sinks" was first published in a collection called *Dionysus-Dithyramben.* In 1891, when the first public edition of the Fourth Part of *Zarathustra* was prepared by Peter Gast, six "Dithyrambs" were appended to it, with a separate half-title and table of contents (23 pages in all), and the following note on the inside front cover: ". . . The Dithyrambs (written in the fall of 1888) that are printed at the end of the book are to be considered as a separate publication, and not as an appendix to this Fourth Part. . . ." In later editions three more poems were added to this collection, all three of them from the Fourth Part of *Zarathustra*, but in some editions with some variants. These are due to the fact that Part Four was completed in 1885, and some of the other "Dithyrambs" belong to that period, too; but the poet later made some changes. "The Sun Sinks," probably written in 1888, is not affected by these changes.

The "Dithyrambs" are very uneven. They were clearly influenced by Hölderlin's late verse, and they in turn influenced Rilke's *Duino Elegies.* But Karl Schlechta seems to be wrong when he claims in the philological postscript of his edition of Nietzsche's *Werke in drei Bänden* that Nietzsche late in 1888 completed a "Druckmanuskript," i.e., a manuscript ready to go to the printer

(Vol. III, 1956, p. 1389). In *Friedrich Nietzsches Werke des Zusammenbruchs* (1961), Erich F. Podach, whose four earlier books made notable contributions to our knowledge of Nietzsche's life, discusses the manuscripts and previous editions of the "Dithyrambs" for over twenty pages—and finds fault with all editions, including Schlechta's. It appears that Nietzsche wrote these poems over a period of four years during which he completed over half a dozen books; but he never got these poems into any final form that fully satisfied him. One version of three of these poems may be found in *The Portable Nietzsche,* pp. 364ff., 409ff., and 416ff., in my translation of *Zarathustra.* Of the others, the one that strikes me as far and away the best is included in the following selections.

Several, but not all, of my translations of Nietzsche's poems appeared originally in my *Nietzsche* (Princeton University Press 1950), in an Appendix, but were omitted in the revised edition, published in paperback by Meridian Books in 1956.

DEM UNBEKANNTEN GOTT

Noch einmal, eh ich weiterziehe
und meine Blicke vorwärts sende,
heb ich vereinsamt meine Hände
zu dir empor, zu dem ich fliehe,
dem ich in tiefster Herzenstiefe
Altäre feierlich geweiht,
dass allezeit
mich deine Stimme wieder riefe.

Darauf erglüht tiefeingeschrieben
das Wort: Dem unbekannten Gotte.
Sein bin ich, ob ich in der Frevler Rotte
auch bis zur Stunde bin geblieben:
sein bin ich–und ich fühl die Schlingen,
die mich im Kampf darniederziehn
und, mag ich fliehn,
mich doch zu seinem Dienste zwingen.

Ich will dich kennen, Unbekannter,
du tief in meine Seele Greifender,
mein Leben wie ein Sturm Durchschweifender,
du Unfassbarer, mir Verwandter!
Ich will dich kennen, selbst dir dienen.

UNVERZAGT

Wo du stehst, grab' tief hinein!
Drunten ist die Quelle!
Lass die dunklen Männer schrein:
„Stets ist drunten–Hölle!"

TO THE UNKNOWN GOD

Once more before I wander on
and turn my eyes to distant lands,
in solitude I raise my hands
to you on high to whom I fly,
whom in my heart's profundity
I hallowed altars to implore
that evermore
your voice might call again to me.

On them is glowing, inscribed deep,
the word: Unto the Unknown God.
His am I, although in the sinners' squad
until this hour I did keep:
his am I, and I feel the chains
that in my fight I can't untie
and, though I fly,
force me to serve the god again.

I want to know you, Unknown One,
you that are reaching deep into my soul
and ravaging my life, a savage gale,
you Inconceivable and yet Related One!
I want to know you—even serve.

UNDAUNTED

Where you stand, dig deep and pry!
Down there is the well.
Let the obscurantists cry:
"Down there's only—hell!"

VADEMECUM—VADETECUM

Es lockt dich meine Art und Sprach,
du folgest mir, du gehst mir nach?
Geh nur dir selber treulich nach:—
so folgst du mir—gemach! gemach!

DER WEISE SPRICHT

Dem Volke fremd und nützlich doch dem Volke,
zieh' ich des Weges, Sonne bald, bald Wolke—
und immer über *diesem Volke!*

ECCE-HOMO

Ja! Ich weiss, woher ich stamme!
Ungesättigt gleich der Flamme
glühe und verzehr ich mich.
Licht wird alles, was ich fasse,
Kohle alles, was ich lasse:
Flamme bin ich sicherlich!

STERNEN-MORAL

Vorausbestimmt zur Sternenbahn,
was geht dich, Stern, das Dunkel an?

Roll selig hin durch diese Zeit!
Ihr Elend sei dir fremd und weit!

VADEMECUM–VADETECUM

Lured by my style and tendency,
you follow and come after me?
Follow your own self faithfully–
take time–and thus you follow me.

THE SAGE SPEAKS

A stranger to the crowd, yet useful to the crowd,
I point a way, now sun and now a cloud–
and always far above the crowd.

ECCE HOMO

Yes, I know from where I came!
Ever hungry like a flame,
I consume myself and glow.
Light grows all that I conceive,
ashes everything I leave:
flame I am assuredly.

STAR MORALS

Called a star's orbit to pursue,
what is the darkness, star, to you?

Roll on in bliss, traverse this age–
its misery far from you and strange.

Der fernsten Welt gehört dein Schein:
Mitleid soll Sünde für dich sein!

Nur Ein Gebot gilt dir: sei rein!

DER EINSAMSTE

Nun, da der Tag
des Tags müde ward, und aller Sehnsucht Bäche
von neuem Trost plätschern,
auch alle Himmel, aufgehängt in Gold-Spinnetzen,
zu jedem Müden sprechen: „Ruhe nun!"
was ruhst du nicht, du dunkles Herz,
was stachelt dich zu fusswunder Flucht . . .
wes harrest du?

AN GOETHE

Das Unvergängliche
ist nur dein Gleichnis!
Gott der Verfängliche
ist Dichter-Erschleichnis . . .

Welt-Rad, das rollende,
streift Ziel auf Ziel:
Not—nennts der Grollende,
der Narr nennts—Spiel . . .

Welt-Spiel, das herrische,
mischt Sein und Schein:—
das Ewig-Närrische
mischt uns hinein! . . .

Let farthest world your light secure.
Pity is sin you must abjure.

But one command is yours: be pure!

THE LONELIEST ONE

Now that the day
grew weary of the day, and all the streams of longing
are splashing of new comfort,
and all the heavens, wrought in golden spiderwebs,
speak to the weary: Rest now!
why don't you rest, dark heart,
what spurs you on to footsore flight—
why do you wait?

TO GOETHE

The indestructible
is but your invention.
God, the ineluctable,
poetic pretension.

World wheel, while rolling on,
skims aim on aim:
Fate, says the sullen one,
fools call it a game.

World game, the ruling force,
blends false and true:
the eternally fooling force
blends us in too.

AN DEN MISTRAL

EIN TANZLIED

Mistral-Wind, du Wolken-Jäger,
Trübsal-Mörder, Himmels-Feger,
brausender, wie lieb ich dich!
Sind wir zwei nicht Eines Schosses
Erstlingsgabe, Eines Loses
Vorbestimmte ewiglich?

Hier auf glatten Felsenwegen
lauf ich tanzend dir entgegen,
tanzend, wie du pfeifst und singst:
der du ohne Schiff und Ruder
als der Freiheit freister Bruder
über wilde Meere springst.

Kaum erwacht, hört ich dein Rufen,
stürmte zu den Felsenstufen,
hin zur gelben Wand am Meer.
Heil! da kamst du schon gleich hellen
diamantnen Stromesschnellen
sieghaft von den Bergen her.

Auf den ebnen Himmels-Tennen
sah ich deine Rosse rennen,
sah den Wagen, der dich trägt,
sah die Hand dir selber zücken,
wenn sie auf der Rosse Rücken
blitzesgleich die Geissel schlägt.–

TO THE MISTRAL

A DANCING SONG

Mistral wind, you rain cloud leaper,
sadness killer, heaven sweeper,
how I love you when you roar!
Were we two not generated
in one womb, predestinated
for one lot for evermore?

Here on slippery rocky traces
I dance into your embraces,
dancing as you sing and whistle:
you that, shipless, do not halt,
freedom's freest brother, vault
over raging seas, a missile.

Barely waked, I heard your calling,
stormed to where the rocks are sprawling,
to the gold wall by the sea—
when you came like swiftly dashing
river rapids, diamond-splashing,
from the peaks triumphantly.

Through the heavens' threshing basin
I could see your horses hasten,
saw the carriage you commanded,
saw your hand yourself attack
when upon the horses' back
lightning-like your scourge descended.

Sah dich aus dem Wagen springen,
schneller dich hinabzuschwingen,
sah dich wie zum Pfeil verkürzt
senkrecht in die Tiefe stossen,—
wie ein Goldstrahl durch die Rosen
erster Morgenröten stürzt.

Tanze nun auf tausend Rücken,
Wellen-Rücken, Wellen-Tücken—
Heil, wer neue *Tänze schafft!*
Tanzen wir in tausend Weisen,
frei—sei unsre *Kunst geheissen,*
fröhlich—unsre *Wissenschaft!*

Raffen wir von jeder Blume
eine Blüte uns zum Ruhme
und zwei Blätter noch zum Kranz!
Tanzen wir gleich Troubadouren
zwischen Heiligen und Huren,
zwischen Gott und Welt den Tanz!

Wer nicht tanzen kann mit Winden,
wer sich wickeln muss mit Binden,
angebunden, Krüppel-Greis,
wer da gleicht den Heuchel-Hänsen,
Ehren-Tölpeln, Tugend-Gänsen,
fort aus unsrem Paradeis!

Wirbeln wir den Staub der Strassen
allen Kranken in die Nasen,
scheuchen wir die Kranken-Brut!
Lösen wir die ganze Küste
von dem Odem dürrer Brüste,
von den Augen ohne Mut!

From your carriage of disaster
leaping to bear down yet faster,
I saw you in arrow form
vertically downward plunging,
like a golden sunbeam lunging
through the roses of the dawn.

Dance on myriad backs a season,
billows' backs and billows' treason—
we need dances that are new!
Let us dance in myriad manners,
freedom write on *our* art's banners,
make our science gay and true.

Let us break from every flower
one fine blossom for our power
and two leaves to wind a wreath!
Let us dance like troubadours
between holy men and whores,
between god and world beneath!

Who thinks tempests dance too quickly,
all the bandaged and the sickly,
crippled, old, and overnice,
if you fear the wind might hurt you,
honor fools and geese of virtue—
out of our paradise!

Let us whirl the dusty hazes
right into the sick men's noses,
flush the sick brood everywhere!
Let us free the coast together
from the wilted bosoms' blether,
from the eyes that never dare!

Jagen wir die Himmels-Trüber,
Welten-Schwärzer, Wolken-Schieber,
hellen wir das Himmelreich!
Brausen wir . . . o aller freien
Geister Geist, mit dir zu zweien
braust *mein Glück dem Sturme gleich.—*

—Und dass ewig das Gedächtnis
solchen Glücks, nimm sein Vermächtnis,
nimm den Kranz *hier mit hinauf!*
Wirf ihn höher, ferner, weiter,
stürm empor die Himmelsleiter,
häng ihn—an den Sternen auf!

VENEDIG

An der Brücke stand
jüngst ich in brauner Nacht.
Fernher kam Gesang:
goldener Tropfen quolls
über die zitternde Fläche weg.
Gondeln, Lichter, Musik—
trunken schwamms in die Dämmrung hinaus . . .

Meine Seele, ein Saitenspiel,
sang sich, unsichtbar berührt,
heimlich ein Gondellied dazu,
zitternd vor bunter Seligkeit.
—Hörte jemand ihr zu? . . .

Let us chase the shadow lovers,
world defamers, rain-cloud shovers—
let us brighten up the sky!
All free spirits' spirit, let you
and me thunder; since I met you,
like a tempest roars my joy.

And forever to attest
such great joy, take its bequest,
take this wreath with you up there!
Toss it higher, further, gladder,
storm up on the heavens' ladder,
hang it up—upon a star.

VENICE

At the bridge of late
I stood in the brown night.
From afar came a song:
as a golden drop it welled
over the quivering surface.
Gondolas, lights, and music—
drunken it swam out into the twilight.

My soul, a stringed instrument,
sang to itself, invisibly touched,
a secret gondola song,
quivering with iridescent happiness.
—Did anyone listen to it?

DIE SONNE SINKT

I

Nicht lange durstest du noch,
verbranntes Herz!
Verheissung ist in der Luft,
aus unbekannten Mündern bläst michs an,
—die grosse Kühle kommt . . .

Meine Sonne stand heiss über mir im Mittage:
seid mir gegrüsst, dass ihr kommt,
ihr plötzlichen Winde,
ihr kühlen Geister des Nachmittags!

Die Luft geht fremd und rein.
Schielt nicht mit schiefem
Verführerblick
die Nacht mich an? . . .
Bleib stark, mein tapfres Herz!
Frag nicht: warum?—

II

Tag meines Lebens!
die Sonne sinkt.
Schon steht die glatte
Flut vergüldet.
Warm atmet der Fels:
schlief wohl zu Mittag
das Glück auf ihm seinen Mittagsschlaf?
In grünen Lichtern
spielt Glück noch der braune Abgrund herauf.

THE SUN SINKS

I

Not long will you thirst,
  burnt out heart!
A promise is in the air,
from unknown lips it blows at me
  —the great chill comes.

My sun stood hot over me at noon—
be welcome that you come,
  you sudden winds,
you chilly spirits of afternoon!

The air moves strange and pure.
Does not with warped
  seductive eyes
night leer at me?
Stay strong, courageous heart!
Do not ask: why?

II

Day of my life!
The sun sinks.
Already the smooth
  flood stands golden.
Warm breathes the rock:
  whether at noon
joy slept its noonday sleep upon it?
  In greenish lights
Joy is still playing over the brown abyss.

Tag meines Lebens!
gen Abend gehts!
Schon glüht dein Auge
  halbgebrochen,
schon quillt deines Taus
  Tränengeträufel,
schon läuft still über weisse Meere
deiner Liebe Purpur,
deine letzte zögernde Seligkeit . . .

III

Heiterkeit, güldene, komm!
  du des Todes
heimlichster, süssester Vorgenuss!
—Lief ich zu rasch meines Wegs?
Jetzt erst, wo der Fuss müde ward,
  holt dein Blick mich noch ein,
  holt dein Glück *mich noch ein.*

Rings nur Welle und Spiel.
  Was je schwer war,
sank in blaue Vergessenheit,—
müssig steht nun mein Kahn.
Sturm und Fahrt—wie verlernt' er das!
  Wunsch und Hoffen ertrank,
  glatt liegt Seele und Meer.

Siebente *Einsamkeit!*
  Nie empfand ich
näher mir süsse Sicherheit,
wärmer der Sonne Blick.
—Glüht nicht das Eis meiner Gipfel noch?
  Silbern, leicht, ein Fisch,
  schwimmt nun mein Nachen hinaus . . .

Day of my life!
Toward evening it goes.
Already your eye
  glows half-broken,
already your dew's
  tear drops are welling,
already runs still over white seas
your love's purple,
your last hesitant blessedness.

III

Cheerfulness, golden one, come!
  you of death
the most secret and sweetest foretaste!
Did I run too rash on my way?
Only now that my foot has grown weary,
  your eye catches up with me,
  your *joy* catches up with me.

Round me but wave and play.
  Whatever was hard
sank into blue oblivion—
idle stands now my boat.
Storm and drive—how it forgot that!
  Wish and hope have drowned,
  smooth lie soul and sea.

Seventh loneliness!
  Never felt I
nearer me sweet security,
warmer the sun's eye.
Does not the ice of my peaks still glow?
  Silver, light, a fish,
  my bark now swims out.

STEFAN GEORGE

(1868-1933)

As was mentioned in the preface to Heine, Stefan George had a most exalted conception of his mission. In the distant past he venerated Dante; more recently, he thought that he had received his prophet's mantle from Nietzsche, to whom he devoted two poems. The first was written in 1900, on the occasion of the philosopher's death, and included in *Der Siebente Ring* (1907, The Seventh Ring). George's conception of Nietzsche—especially the lines beginning "Didst thou create gods but to overthrow them . . ."—influenced not only such George disciples as the brothers Gundolf (Friedrich and Ernst) and Ernst Bertram (whose *Nietzsche: Versuch einer Mythologie,* i.e., "Attempt at a Mythology," 1918, was for at least fifteen years by far the most influential interpretation) but also, albeit indirectly, Karl Jaspers' *Nietzsche.* Jaspers finds Nietzsche's alleged destruction of *all* positions an ideal introduction to his own *Existenzphilosophie.* George found in it a limitation of the philosopher that marked him as a mere herald of one greater than himself, one who was not a mere philosopher, one who understood what was needed as Nietzsche, alas, did not. As Kurt Hildebrandt put it in *Nietzsche als Richter unserer Zeit* (1923, Nietzsche as

Judge of our Time): "Only George *is* what Nietzsche convulsively coveted to be." Or as George himself put it in his poem in 1900: "Now this is needed: constraint within a circle." Instead of going it alone "over icy cliffs," one must found a circle, the so-called *George Kreis,* in which the poet sought to bring together the most promising young men of the next generation in order that he might regenerate Germany and the world through their work and his. As he said in one of his poems: "In jeder ewe / Ist nur ein gott und einer nur sein künder" (In every epoch is but one god, and only one his prophet). The prophet must not speak but sing; but to enhance his effect on the deaf mass, his minions might translate his inspired music into prose. The conclusion of the poem on "Nietzsche" was almost a straight quote from Nietzsche's own preface (1886) to the second edition of *The Birth of Tragedy,* originally published in 1872: "It should have *sung,* this 'new soul'—and not spoken!"

The other three George poems come from *Der Stern des Bundes* (1914, The Star of the Covenant). In the original, none bears a title; but it was known from the start, and there is general agreement, that the first of these again refers to Nietzsche. All four of the poems offered here give some idea of George's world view.

Not only his outlook was aristocratic, but the form of his verse, too, was deliberately opposed to everything lax, popular, unrefined. To set it off from the verse of others, even in appearance, George capitalized only the first word in each line or sentence and, of course, proper names, but not, as is general practice in modern German, every noun. Much more important:

a great deal of his verse is distinguished by a rare nobility.

After Hitler came to power, in 1933, Stefan George was offered the presidency of the *Deutsche Dichterakademie,* but sent one of the Jewish members of the Circle to inform Goebbels of his refusal, and left for Switzerland. Bertram, Hildebrandt, and others who had been more or less close to the Circle became Nazis. Friedrich Gundolf was dead. Karl Wolfskehl, who had been especially close to George, emigrated, being a Jew. George made no statements. In December he died in Locarno and, in accordance with his wishes, was buried there, in Switzerland. Two brothers, Counts Stauffenberg, kept a death watch before the interment. Ten years later, one of them commemorated the anniversary of George's death with a cycle of poems. Seven months later, on July 20, 1944, the other brother planted the bomb that was meant to kill Hitler.

All of George's poems are most conveniently consulted in Stefan George: *Werke in zwei Bänden,* Verlag Helmut Küpper vormals Georg Bondi, Düsseldorf · München. The four poems that follow are reproduced with the publisher's kind permission.

NIETZSCHE

Schwergelbe wolken ziehen überm hügel
Und kühle stürme—halb des herbstes boten
Halb frühen frühlings . . . Also diese mauer
Umschloss den Donnerer—ihn der einzig war
Von tausenden aus rauch und staub um ihn?
Hier sandte er auf flaches mittelland
Und tote stadt die lezten stumpfen blitze
Und ging aus langer nacht zur längsten nacht.

Blöd trabt die menge drunten • scheucht sie nicht!
Was wäre stich der qualle • schnitt dem kraut
Noch eine weile walte fromme stille
Und das getier das ihn mit lob befleckt
Und sich im moderdunste weiter mästet
Der ihn erwürgen half sei erst verendet!
Dann aber stehst du strahlend vor den zeiten
Wie andre führer mit der blutigen krone.

Erlöser du! selbst der unseligste—
Beladen mit der wucht von welchen losen
Hast du der sehnsucht land nie lächeln sehn?
Erschufst du götter nur um sie zu stürzen
Nie einer rast und eines baues froh?
Du hast das nächste in dir selbst getötet
Um neu begehrend dann ihm nachzuzittern
Und aufzuschrein im schmerz der einsamkeit.

NIETZSCHE

Over the hill drift heavy yellow clouds
and chilling gales—half messengers of autumn
and half of early spring. So this wall here
enclosed the thunderer—him that had no peer
among the thousands, smoke and dust about him?
Here he dispatched on the flat middle land
and the dead town the final blunted lightnings
and went from his long night to longest night.

Dull trots the crowd below, do not disturb it!
Why stab the jelly-fish or cut the weed?
For a while yet let pious silence reign,
and let the vermin that stain him with praise
and are still fattening on the musty fumes
that helped to stifle him, first waste away!
But then, resplendent, thou wilt face the ages
like other leaders with the bloody crown.

Redeemer thou! thyself the most unblessed—
bearing the burden of what destinies
were you denied the smile of longing's land?
Didst thou create gods but to overthrow them,
never enjoying rest or what thou built?
Thou hast destroyed what in thyself was closest
to tremble after it with new desire
and to cry out in pain of solitude.

Der kam zu spät der flehend zu dir sagte:
Dort ist kein weg mehr über eisige felsen
Und horste grauser vögel–nun ist not:
Sich bannen in den kreis den liebe schliesst . .
Und wenn die strenge und gequälte stimme
Dann wie ein loblied tönt in blaue nacht
Und helle flut–so klagt: sie hätte singen
Nicht reden sollen diese neue seele!

AUS „DER STERN DES BUNDES"

Einer stand auf der scharf wie blitz und stahl
Die klüfte aufriss und die lager schied
Ein Drüben schuf durch umkehr eures Hier . .
Der euren wahnsinn so lang in euch schrie
Mit solcher wucht dass ihm die kehle barst.
Und ihr? ob dumpf ob klug ob falsch ob echt
Vernahmt und saht als wäre nichts geschehn . .
Ihr handelt weiter sprecht und lacht und heckt.
Der warner ging . . dem rad das niederrollt
Zur leere greift kein arm mehr in die speiche.

He came too late that said to thee imploring:
there is no way left over icy cliffs
and eyries of dread birds—now this is needed:
constraint within a circle closed by love.
And when the harsh tormented voice resounds,
a song of praise, into the azure night
and brilliant flood—lament: it should have sung,
not spoken, this new soul.

ANOTHER POEM ON NIETZSCHE

One man arose who, sharp as lightning, cracked
open the clefts and, steel-like, severed camps,
creating a Beyond, inverting your old Here—
who roared your madness into you so long
with so much force that his throat burst. And you?
Some dumb, some clever, false or genuine,
perceived and looked as if nothing had happened.—
You go on speaking, laughing, and conspiring.
The warner went—the wheel that hurtles down
toward emptiness no arm attempts to tackle.

AUS „DER STERN DES BUNDES“

Wer je die flamme umschritt
Bleibe der flamme trabant!
Wie er auch wandert und kreist:
Wo noch ihr schein ihn erreicht
Irrt er zu weit nie vom ziel.
Nur wenn sein blick sie verlor
Eigener schimmer ihn trügt:
Fehlt ihm der mitte gesetz
Treibt er zerstiebend ins all.

AUS „DER STERN DES BUNDES“

Ein wissen gleich für alle heisst betrug.
Drei sind des wissens grade. Eines steigt
Aus dumpfer menge ahndung: keim und brut
In alle wache rege eures stamms.
Das zweite bringt der zeiten buch und schule.
Das dritte führt nur durch der weihe tor.
Drei sind der wisser stufen. Nur der wahn
Meint dass er die durchspringt: geburt und leib.
Die andre gleichen zwangs ist schaun und fassen.
Die letzte kennt nur wen der gott beschlief.

[WHO EVER]

Who ever circled the flame
has to remain its vassal!
Though he may roam and stray:
where he is reached by its splendor,
he has not erred too far.
But when his eye has lost it
and his own light deceives him:
lacking the law of the center
he is dispersed and scattered.

[ONE LORE]

One lore equal for all is an illusion;
three are the grades of knowledge. One ascends
from the dull masses' notions: germ and breeding
in every waking stirring of your tribe.
The book and school of ages brings the second.
The third is found by the initiate only.
Three are the knowers' stages. But conceit
believes that one can skip: body and birth.
The other equal force: seeing and grasping.
The last knows only whom the god impregnates.

HUGO VON HOFMANNSTHAL

(1874-1929)

Hofmannsthal was born in Vienna. Some of his best work was written before he was twenty; for example, his short verse dramas, *Der Tod des Tizian* (1892, The Death of Titian) and *Der Tor und der Tod* (1900, The Fool and Death). These plays, like most of his poems, which were also written in the nineties, are distinguished by their languid beauty. But in *Der Tor und der Tod,* which leans heavily on the opening monologues of Goethe's *Faust,* the weariness of the *fin de siècle* is given an existentialist twist. Confronted with death, the fool recognizes the emptiness and futility of his uncommitted life. After listening to three of the dead—his mother, a girl who loved him, and a former friend whose speech is especially fine—Claudio, the fool, welcomes death: "Only as I die, I feel that I am." And Death comments in the last speech of the play: "How strange are these beings who still find a meaning in what is meaningless."

The preoccupation with man's confrontation of death is continued in the best known play of the poet's maturity, *Jedermann* (1911, Everyman), which deals with the death of the rich man. It is annually performed in Salzburg as part of the *Festspiele.*

Hofmannsthal, who was half Jewish by descent, died before the Nazis came to power in Germany—in 1929, shortly after his son's suicide. His reputation at that time rested largely on the works mentioned and on the many librettos he had written for Richard Strauss. Since then critical opinion has changed, and some of his later works have come to be appreciated more, especially his late tragedy, *Der Turm* (1925, revised version 1927; The Tower), and some of his criticism.

Stefan George was among the first to recognize his genius—he had begun to publish at sixteen—and befriended the precocious youth. Yet Hofmannsthal was much too independent to submit to the iron will of the older poet who liked to mold men as well as language; and in 1906 the two broke permanently.

The poems that follow are reproduced with the permission of the S. Fischer Verlag, Frankfurt am Main.

DIE BEIDEN

Sie trug den Becher in der Hand,
—ihr Kinn und Mund glich seinem Rand—,
So leicht und sicher war ihr Gang,
Kein Tropfen aus dem Becher sprang.

So leicht und fest war seine Hand:
Er ritt auf einem jungen Pferde,
Und mit nachlässiger Gebärde
Erzwang er, dass es zitternd stand.

Jedoch, wenn er aus ihrer Hand
Den leichten Becher nehmen sollte,
So war es beiden allzuschwer:
Denn beide bebten sie so sehr,
Dass keine Hand die andre fand
Und dunkler Wein am Boden rollte.

BALLADE DES ÄUSSEREN LEBENS

Und Kinder wachsen auf mit tiefen Augen,
Die von nichts wissen, wachsen auf und sterben,
Und alle Menschen gehen ihre Wege.

Und süsse Früchte werden aus den herben
Und fallen nachts wie tote Vögel nieder
Und liegen wenig Tage und verderben.

THE TWO

She bore the goblet in her hand–
her chin and mouth firm as its band–
her stride so weightless and so still
that not a drop would ever spill.

So weightless and so firm his hand:
he rode a young horse for his pleasure
and, looking like incarnate leisure,
compelled it; trembling it must stand.

But when he should take from her hand
the goblet that she lifted up,
the two were quivering so much
that each hand missed the other's touch,
and heavy grew the weightless cup
till dark wine rolled upon the sand.

BALLAD OF OUTER LIFE

And children grow up slowly with deep eyes,
that know of nothing; they grow up and toil
and die, and all men walk their ways.

And bitter fruit grow sweet, drop to the soil
at night, exhausted, like dead birds,
and lie a few days on the ground and spoil.

Und immer weht der Wind, und immer wieder
Vernehmen wir und reden viele Worte
Und spüren Lust und Müdigkeit der Glieder.

Und Strassen laufen durch das Gras, und Orte
Sind da und dort, voll Fackeln, Bäumen, Teichen,
Und drohende, und totenhaft verdorrte . . .

Wozu sind diese aufgebaut? und gleichen
Einander nie? und sind unzählig viele?
Was wechselt Lachen, Weinen und Erbleichen?

Was frommt das alles uns und diese Spiele,
Die wir doch gross und ewig einsam sind
Und wandernd nimmer suchen irgend Ziele?

Was frommt's, dergleichen viel gesehen haben?
Und dennoch sagt der viel, der „Abend" sagt,
Ein Wort, daraus Tiefsinn und Trauer rinnt

Wie schwerer Honig aus den hohlen Waben.

And always blows the wind, and always words
are heard and spoken as we blether,
and pleasantness and weariness recur.

And roads run through the grass hither and thither,
and there are towns with streetlights, ponds, and trees,
and some look threatening, others, deathlike, wither.

For what are these built? and for what are these
endlessly many? and no two the same?
Why always laughter, weeping, and decease?

What good to us is all this and these games,
when we are great, alone eternally,
and wandering never pursue any aims?

What good is it to have seen much such folly?
And yet he says much that says "evening,"
a word from which meaning and melancholy

issue like honey out of hollow combs.

CHRISTIAN MORGENSTERN

(1871-1914)

◇◇

Morgenstern's work is conveniently divided into three genres. He was a lyrical poet and published several collections, including *Melancholie* (1906), *Ich und Du* (1911), and *Wir fanden einen Pfad* (1914, We Found a Path). He wrote epigrams, collected in *Stufen* (1918, Steps) and *Epigramme und Sprüche* (1920, Epigrams and Apothegms). The four epigrams that follow come from the latter volume and were written in the late nineties. But he is best known for his incomparable *Galgenlieder* (Gallows Songs).

Originally, these appeared in four volumes: *Galgenlieder* (1905), *Palmström* (1910), *Palma Kunkel* (1916), and *Gingganz* (1919). Later all these poems were collected in *Alle Galgenlieder,* and some previously unpublished material was added. The motto was taken from Nietzsche's *Zarathustra:* "In a real man a child is hidden—and wants to play." Indeed, there is a good deal in *Zarathustra* that is quite close in spirit to Morgenstern's *Galgenlieder.*

Morgenstern's "Attempt at an Introduction," signed by a fictitious "Jeremias Müller, Lic. Dr.," is a delightful parody of pretentious German prose: the last sentence takes up more than half a page, contains a word that takes up almost an entire line, and ends with a preposterous assembly of verbs. Then there is a preface, entitled "How the Gallows Songs originated." It is only a page long and consists largely of a somewhat surrealistic fairy tale. The last sentence reads: "From the gallows one looks differently at the world and sees different things than others."

The four epigrams are reproduced with the permission of R. Piper et Co. Verlag, München, the publisher of *Epigramme und Sprüche,* while the three longer poems are printed with the permission of Insel-Verlag, Frankfurt am Main, publisher of *Alle Galgenlieder.*

AN NIETZSCHE

Mag die Torheit durch dich fallen,
mir, mir warst du Brot und Wein,
und was mir, das wirst du allen
meinesgleichen sein.

DER GELEHRTE UND GOETHE

‚Ich weiss, was er zu jeder Zeit gesagt,
doch mein Gewissen hat er nie geplagt.'

[L'ART POUR L'ART]

L'art pour l'art, das heisst so viel:
Wir haben nur noch Kraft zum Spiel.

DER SPARSAME DICHTER

‚Willst du nicht Artikel schreiben?'—
Lasst's beim Epigramme bleiben.
Kann ich's euch in zehn Zeilen sagen,
was euch verwundert,
warum euch Honorar abjagen
für hundert.

PALMSTRÖM

Palmström steht an einem Teiche
Und entfaltet gross ein rotes Taschentuch:
Auf dem Tuch ist eine Eiche
dargestellt sowie ein Mensch mit einem Buch.

TO NIETZSCHE

Folly you may lead to fall;
for me you were bread and wine.
What you gave me you'll give all
who are of my kind.

THE SCHOLAR AND GOETHE

Whatever date you name, I know the text;
my conscience, though, he never vexed.

L'ART POUR L'ART

L'art pour l'art, that is to say:
We've only strength enough to play.

THE ECONOMICAL POET

"Write an article," suggests a letter.
Thank you, epigrams suit me far better.
If in ten lines I can say
what makes you wonder,
why should I ask you to pay
for a hundred?

PALMSTRÖM

Palmström, standing at a lake,
opens a huge handkerchief and takes a look:
on it he beholds an oak
pictured and a man who holds a book.

Palmström wagt nicht, sich hineinzuschneuzen.
Er gehört zu jenen Käuzen,
die oft unvermittelt-nackt
Ehrfurcht vor dem Schönen packt.

Zärtlich faltet er zusammen,
was er eben erst entbreitet.
Und kein Fühlender wird ihn verdammen,
weil er ungeschneuzt entschreitet.

DIE UNMÖGLICHE TATSACHE

Palmström, etwas schon an Jahren,
wird an einer Strassenbeuge
und von einem Kraftfahrzeuge
überfahren.

„Wie war" (spricht er, sich erhebend
und entschlossen weiterlebend)
„möglich, wie dies Unglück, ja—:
dass es überhaupt geschah?

Ist die Staatskunst anzuklagen
in bezug auf Kraftfahrwagen?
Gab die Polizeivorschrift
hier dem Fahrer freie Trift?

Oder war vielmehr verboten,
hier Lebendige zu Toten
umzuwandeln,—kurz und schlicht:
D u r f t e hier der Kutscher nicht—?"

Palmström does not dare to blow his nose,
for he happens to be one of those
seizable at any time
by regard for the sublime.

Tenderly, he folds again
what but now we had been shown;
and no feeling heart will damn
him that strides off, nose unblown.

THE IMPOSSIBLE FACT

Palmström, strolling through the town,
tried to cross the bending road
when an automobile mowed
him down.

"How was (says he, still alive
and resolving to survive)
possible this mishap—or
could it really occur?

Is our statecraft here at fault
anent motorized assault?
Did the police regulation
give the driver a vacation?

Or was it against the norm
at this corner to transform
living men to dead condition:
did this driver lack permission?"

Eingehüllt in feuchte Tücher,
prüft er die Gesetzesbücher
und ist alsobald im klaren:
Wagen durften dort nicht fahren!

Und er kommt zu dem Ergebnis:
„Nur ein Traum war das Erlebnis.
Weil", so schliesst er messerscharf,
„nicht sein k a n n, was nicht sein d a r f."

DIE BRILLE

Korf liest gerne schnell und viel;
darum widert ihn das Spiel
all des zwölfmal unerbetnen
Ausgewalzten, Breitgetretnen.

Meistes ist in sechs bis acht
Wörtern völlig abgemacht,
und in ebensoviel Sätzen
lässt sich Bandwurmweisheit schwätzen.

Es erfindet drum sein Geist
etwas, was ihn dem entreisst:
Brillen, deren Energieen
ihm den Text—zusammenziehen!

Beispielsweise dies Gedicht
läse, so bebrillt, man—nicht!
Dreiunddreissig seinesgleichen
gäben erst—Ein—Fragezeichen!!

Wrapped in towels, he consults
law books and finds the results
beyond any question clear:
cars were not permitted here.

And he reaches the conclusion
that the mishap was illusion.
For, he argues razor-witted,
that *can't* be which is not permitted.

THE GLASSES

Korf reads much, and he is quick;
hence it simply makes him sick
to find endless repetitions
and vast over-expositions.

Most points, he finds, can be made
in six words, at most in eight;
and in sentences that number
one can lead tapeworms to slumber.

He invents, sad and perplexed,
an ideal remedy:
spectacles whose energy
will condense a longish text.

Would one have to read this poem with glasses like this? No!
Thirty-three like this would—hark!—
yield a single question mark!!

RAINER MARIA RILKE

(1875-1926)

As an undergraduate I still considered Rilke one among many fine German poets and felt that he was overestimated in the English-speaking world. But the longer I have lived with his poems, reading them again and again and translating some of them, the more I am persuaded that no other poet since Goethe has written so many superb poems. I mention this partly because Rilke's unparalleled vogue among young women may create the presumption that a mature taste should outgrow him.

Still, I have two reservations about him. The poems that are widely considered his greatest achievement and have elicited the largest body of interpretations, commentaries, and criticism, his *Duino Elegies,* still seem somewhat overrated to me, especially in relation to his other poems. There is no reason for disparaging them, but there is a growing tendency to measure greatness by the weight and bulk of secondary literature and to underrate simple excellence, however profound, in favor of whatever is obscure, difficult, long, and in need of explanation. The point is not to deny the beauty of the elegies but rather to praise his shorter poems much more than is usual.

The other reservation concerns the man behind the poems and the unusually large body of his letters. While Heine strikes me as a world-historical figure whose significance is insufficiently suggested by a few of his poems, no matter which, Rilke seems a much less significant human being, and his letters, in which he takes himself far too seriously and often poses as a sage, do not add to his stature. Many are interesting, many embarrassing. To put it differently and a little too simply: his lack of a sense of humor does not mar his poems but seems a defect in the man. He was not a human archetype like Goethe and Hölderlin, Heine and Nietzsche. But his poems constitute one of the greatest treasures of world literature.

The first of those that follow, "Rabbi Loew," has been included only for its historical interest. It was one of his earliest poems, included in his first volume of verse, *Larenopfer* (1895); and it shows how he, too, had to learn his craft. The poem contains two Hebrew words: the "bocher" is a young man, a student; and "Beth Chaim," literally house of life, means cemetery.

The verses addressed "To Stephan [*sic*] George" (winter 1897–98) start well enough, but soon become mannered to the point where they approximate parody, and throughout the alliterations are on the heavy side. Here, of course, the interest resides in large measure in the contents: Rilke tells us why, although he, too, abhors vulgarity, he does not feel drawn toward George. The older poet's world seems too solemn and pale for his taste, indeed frozen and lifeless. He is looking for something softer and less willful. The last five lines, which at first reading are apt to seem obscure, strike a theme encountered again in Rilke's last poems, especially in the third sonnet to Orpheus (found later in this volume: "A god can do it . . ."). George's approach, spreading his arms like a hierophant expecting a revelation that he has tried to invoke with his spells and charms, spoils the inspiration that might have come. His domineering will ensures verses as cold as ice.

"The Song of the Idiot" comes from *Das Buch der Bilder* (1903, The Book of Images). Rilke's *Bilder* (pictures or images) are not severe and frozen but attempts to penetrate the heart of what he sees. The same is true of most of the poems from the two volumes of *Neue Gedichte* (1907/08, New Poems) that follow. All the poems from "Love Song" through "Buddha in the Glory" come from these two collections. "Song" is from his only major prose work, *Die Aufzeichnungen des Malte Laurids Brigge* (1910, The Notes of Malte Laurids Brigge). The ten *Duino Elegies*, of which only the ninth is included here, and the *Sonnets to Orpheus* were originally published in 1923. The three poems that conclude the Rilke selections were written during the last three years of the poet's life and published posthumously.

My translations of some of these poems appeared originally in two essays on "Nietzsche and Rilke" and "Art, Tradition, and Truth"—first in *The Kenyon Review* and *Partisan Review* (both Winter 1955), then in my book, *From Shakespeare to Existentialism* (Chapters 12 and 13). There I have also offered detailed discussions of the following poems: "The Song of the Idiot," "Love Song," "The Panther," "Archaic Torso of Apollo," the three Sonnets to Orpheus, and Rilke's last poem—

and these two chapters should also facilitate the understanding of the other poems.

"Roman Fountain" invites comparison with Meyer's poem on the same theme, found earlier in this volume; "Leda," with Yeats' "Leda and the Swan," which was written later, in 1923.

Many, but by no means all, of these poems are available in other translations. Mine were made independently, but I have found it interesting to compare them afterwards. Two of the poems selected here have also been "imitated" by Robert Lowell, who says in the Introduction to his *Imitations* (1961): "I have been reckless with literal meaning, and labored hard to get the tone." No reader is likely to quarrel with the first part of that statement. What is interesting, however, is the widespread assumption that bold departures from the original are all but indispensable "to get the tone." Consider the long poem on Orpheus and Eurydice. Lowell's version appears not only in his *Imitations* but also in Flores's *An Anthology of German Poetry from Hölderlin to Rilke*. It ends:

> [Hermes] pushed off again.
> His caduceus was like a shotgun on his shoulder.

Lowell has also imitated Rilke's last poem, calling it "Pigeons" and adding a stanza in which Leonidas' Spartan soldiers "combed one another's golden Botticellian hair," being "friends and lovers," before they "moved into position to die." Presumably this is meant to illustrate the idea that the experience of danger can make gentle. The last line of this "imitation" features a triple alliteration and ends "mania to return."

One of the themes that runs through Rilke's verse, from beginning to end, is the repudiation of any "mania to return"—or to do anything at all. This point is made most clearly in the first of the three Sonnets to Orpheus that have been included here, especially in the last two lines. Selden Rodman's translation of the final word as "gale" instead of "breeze" misses the point. The young Rilke is a poet of "soft solitudes" and "incense clouds," who shrinks from Stefan George's willfulness. The image of a ball that is thrown, passively, intrigues him. He celebrates the Buddha in three poems (two of them included here)—poems in praise of a state of being that is beyond all agitation. In Rilke's vision even the Roman Fountain has a gentle, peaceful smile. His Eurydice is "uncertain, soft, and void of all impatience"—and these are the concluding words of *his* poem. (Does a "shotgun," even if it does alliterate, help to catch that tone?) The challenge to change our life comes from an archaic torso that has a perfection quite lacking in the mania of our lives. Even in "Leda" this theme is present. Yeats' sonnet has a powerful last line: "Before the indifferent beak could let her drop?" But while in Yeats all is over as the passion is spent, Rilke's sonnet characteristically reaches its climax after the sexual climax, after the release of passion. In the Sonnet to Orpheus that begins "Choose to be changed," Rilke again depreciates hardness and extols unreserved, utterly abandoned openness—symbolized, in the final word, by the wind.

In one of the two poems of 1924, written a year after the Sonnets and two years before his death, "Winged enchantment . . . ," Rilke says that it won't do "merely" to be borne, merely to drift, entirely passive; but the great miracle he celebrates is still "an achievement, granted and unstrained." We must practice and develop our powers to be ready for the gift of grace; we must help by being ready, by having prepared ourselves, by being available, by not having sought premature refuge in some hard shell.

"As nature leaves . . ." has been interpreted at length by Martin Heidegger (*Holzwege,* 1952) who, characteristically, finds the message of the poem where Rilke left four dots. But there is no need to interpolate; Rilke says what he wants to say—and, being a great poet, says it better than his commentators. Taken one at a time, his late poems are extremely "dense" in the sense suggested in the introduction to this volume—in other words, they are at opposite poles from Heidegger's exceedingly prolix prose. A few of Rilke's phrases and lines are captivating even at first reading, and to understand the poems one rarely requires more than three things: one has to read some of these poems several times and live with them for a while; one has to read them in the context of Rilke's other poems, which provide the best commentary there is; and then the poems gradually become clear—unless one lacks the experience of which they speak. But if that is the case, a commentary would be almost as ill advised as explaining love poems to children.

"As nature leaves . . ." develops the theme we have been following. There is no hiding place, no protection; living means being in danger; and man may even "will this venture." Precisely this decision to "live dangerously" is, as Nietzsche put it when he coined this phrase in *The Gay Science* (Section 283), "the secret of the greatest fruitfulness and the greatest enjoyment of existence." Rilke, like Nietzsche before him, associates it with an ultimate affirmation of life.

In the last poem the image of the ball recurs conjoined with the idea of daring. Those who have hidden, "always most protected," have missed out on what is best. Those who have lived dangerously and experienced terror may not look different afterwards, but they *are* different.

The difficulty of these poems does not lie in the presence of allusions and other matters that are conveniently elucidated in footnotes or seminars; it is a matter of rare experiences. Since these experiences are the subject of other literary masterpieces, too, one can, of course, refer to other books; for example, to the concluding pages of *Nietzsche contra Wagner* (a complete translation may be found in *The Portable Nietzsche*). Apart from life itself, nothing is so apt to help us understand Rilke's verse as some acquaintance with Goethe, Hölderlin, and Nietzsche. Not only the translations but also the context provided by *Twenty German Poets* should offer some illumination.

The most complete German edition of Rilke's works is *Sämtliche Werke*, published by the Insel-Verlag. The first volume contains all the poems that Rilke himself collected in books, from *Larenopfer* (1895) to *Sonette an Orpheus* (1923). The second volume offers what else remains of Rilke's verse written during the years from 1906 to 1926, along with the poems he wrote in French. The third volume contains his early verse, written before 1906. Each of these volumes runs about 900 pages and features helpful notes as well as superb indices; and wherever possible the exact dates of composition are given. Volumes four and five are devoted to Rilke's prose.

Of the poems that follow, the last three are found in Volume II; the poem to George, in Volume III; all the others, in Volume I. The kind permission of the Insel-Verlag, and also of W. W. Norton & Company, New York, Rilke's first major publisher in the United States, is gratefully acknowledged.

RABBI LÖW

1

„Weiser Rabbi, hoher Liva, hilf uns aus dem Bann der Not;
heut gibt uns Jehova Kinder, morgen raubt sie uns der Tod.
Schon fasst Beth Chaim nicht die Scharen, und kaum hat der Leichenwart
eins bestattet, nahen andre Tote; Rabbi, das ist hart.“
Und der Rabbi: „Geht und schickt mir einen Bocher rasch herein.“–
So geschiehts: „Wagst du nach Beth Chaim diese Nacht dich ganz allein?“
„Du befiehlst es, weiser Meister?“ „Gut, so hör, um Mitternacht
tanzen all die Kindergeister auf den grauen Steinen sacht.
Birg dich dorten im Gebete, und wenn Furcht dein Herz beklemmt,
streif sie ab: Du raubst dem nächsten Kinde kühn sein Leichenhemd,
raubst es,–bringst es her im Fluge, her zu mir! Begreifst du wohl?“
„Wie du heissest tun mich, Meister, tu ich!“ klingt die Antwort hohl.

2

Mitternacht und Mondgegleisse,–
. . . und es stürzt der totenblasse
Bocher bebend durch die Gasse,
in der Hand das Hemd, das weisse.

RABBI LOEW

1

"Sage and rabbi, stoop to help us from the ban of our sorrow;
though Jehovah gives us children, death takes all of them tomorrow.
Beth Chaim does not hold their hosts, and as soon as Beth Chaim's guard
buries one come other dead ones; rabbi, that is hard."
Says the rabbi: "Get a bocher, send him here and don't postpone."
It is done. "Tonight to Beth Chaim—dare you go there all alone?"
"You command it, sage and rabbi?" "Good, so hear: at twelve o'clock
all the children's sprites are dancing softly on the silver rock.
There you hide yourself in prayer, and if fear should disconcert
you, be brave, approach the nearest child and steal its little shirt—
steal it, bring it here aflying, here to me. Now, do you follow?"
"As you say I do, my master," sounds the bocher's answer hollow.

2

Midnight, yet the moon is bright,
and the bocher, deadly pallid,
dashes, trembling, through the alley,
in his hand the shirt so white.

Da jetzt . . . sind das seine Schritte? . . .
Jach kehrt er zurück das bleiche
Antlitz: Weh, die Kindesleiche
folgt ihm nach, im Aug die Bitte:

„. . . Gib das Linnen, ohne Linnen
lassen mich nicht ein die Geister . . .“
Und der Bocher, halb von Sinnen,
reicht es endlich seinem Meister.

Und schon naht der Geist mit Klagen . . .
„Sag, was sterben hundert binnen
Tagen?–Kind, du musst es sagen,
früher darfst du nicht von hinnen.“

So der Rabbi.–„Wehe, wehe,“
ruft der Geist, „aus unserm Stamme
haben zwei entehrt der Ehe
keusche, reine Altarflamme!

Hier die Namen!–Sucht nicht fremde
Ursach, dass euch Tod beschieden . . .“
Und der Rabbi reicht das Hemde
jetzt dem Kinde: „Zieh in Frieden!“

3

Kaum, dass aus dem Nachtkelch maijung
stieg der Tag in rosgem Licht,
hielt der Rabbi schon Gericht,–
und der Unschuld ward Befreiung.

There—he hears another's pace,
and he turns around, all pale,
sees a child and hears it wail
with this plea writ in its face:

"Give the shroud! Without my shroud"—
crazed with fear he runs but faster—
"to return I'm not allowed"—
and he hands it to his master.

And the sprite comes, too, in sorrow.
"Say, why do a hundred die
within days? You must comply
or I keep you till the morrow."

Thus the rabbi.—"Woe, oh woe,
two of our tribe," it falters,
"stained the chaste and holy glow
of the light on wedlock's altars.

Here, the names.—Don't search the clouds
for the cause of our decease."
And the rabbi hands the shrouds
to the child: "Leave, then, in peace."

3

Hardly had the morning's steed
soared from darkness, golden-feathered,
when the rabbi's court had gathered
and the innocent were freed.

Mit der Geissel des Gesetzes
brandmarkt er die Sünderstirn;–
langsam löste jedes Hirn
sich vom Bann des Fluchgenetzes.

Manches Paar war da erschienen,
dankerfüllt, dass Gott verzieh,
und der Weise segnet sie.–
Freude lag auf aller Mienen.

Nur der Bocher warf, der bleiche,
sich im Fieber hin und her . . .
Doch nach Beth Chaim lange mehr
trug man keine Kindesleiche.

AN STEPHAN GEORGE

Wenn ich, wie du, mich nie den Märkten menge
und leiser Einsamkeiten Segen suche,–
ich werde nie mich neigen vor der Strenge
der bleichen Bilder in dem tiefen Buche.

Sie sind erstarrt in ihren Dämmernischen,
und ihre Stirnen schweigen deinen Schwüren,
nur wenn des Weihrauchs Wellen sie verwischen,
scheint ihrer Lippen Lichte sich zu rühren.

Doch, dass die Seele dann dem Offenbaren
die Arme breitet, wird ihr Lächeln lähmen;
sie werden wieder die sie immer waren:
Kalt wachsen ihre alabasterklaren
Gestalten aus der scheuen Arme Schämen.

With the scourging law he brands
openly the sinners' forehead,
and the curse is gone, the deadly
net is torn like paper bands.

Full of thanks because the Lord
had forgiven, many came
whom the sage blessed in His Name.—
Happiness was thus restored.

But the bocher in his room
lay in fever, white and harried . . .
Yet for years they never carried
children's bodies to the tomb.

TO STEPHAN GEORGE

Though I, like you, don't crowd the marketplaces
but seek the blessing of soft solitudes,
I'll never bow before the solemn faces
in the pale pictures of a book that broods.

They are long frozen in their twilit niches,
their foreheads remain silent to your charms;
only when incense clouds them and bewitches
the stony lips, their light appears to stir.

But when the soul spreads out its eager arms
for revelation, smiles are paralyzed,
and they return to what they always were:
their shapes, as clear as alabaster, rise
out of the shame of the shy arms like ice.

DAS LIED DES IDIOTEN

Sie hindern mich nicht. Sie lassen mich gehn.
Sie sagen es könne nichts geschehn.
Wie gut.
Es kann nichts geschehn. Alles kommt und kreist
immerfort um den heiligen Geist,
um den gewissen Geist (du weisst)–,
wie gut.

Nein man muss wirklich nicht meinen es sei
irgend eine Gefahr dabei.
Da ist freilich das Blut.
Das Blut ist das Schwerste. Das Blut ist schwer.
Manchmal glaub ich, ich kann nicht mehr–.
(Wie gut.)

Ah was ist das für ein schöner Ball;
rot und rund wie ein Überall.
Gut, dass ihr ihn erschuft.
Ob der wohl kommt wenn man ruft?

Wie sich das alles seltsam benimmt,
ineinandertreibt, auseinanderschwimmt:
freundlich, ein wenig unbestimmt.
Wie gut.

LIEBES-LIED

Wie soll ich meine Seele halten, dass
sie nicht an deine rührt? Wie soll ich sie

THE SONG OF THE IDIOT

They do not hinder me. They let me go.
They say, nothing could happen even so.
How good.
Nothing can happen. Everything revolves engrossed
always around the Holy Ghost,
around a certain ghost (you know)—
how good.

No, one really should not suppose
that there is any danger in those.
There's of course the blood.
The blood is the hardest thing. The blood is a chore,
sometimes I think I can't any more.
(How good.)

Look at that ball, isn't it fair—
red and round as an everywhere.
Good you created the ball.
Whether it comes when we call?

How oddly all things seem to humor some whim,
they flock together, apart they swim,
friendly and just a little dim;
how good.

LOVE SONG

How could I keep my soul so that it might
not touch on yours? How could I elevate

hinheben über dich zu andern Dingen?
Ach gerne möcht ich sie bei irgendwas
Verlorenem im Dunkel unterbringen
an einer fremden stillen Stelle, die
nicht weiterschwingt, wenn deine Tiefen schwingen.
Doch alles, was uns anrührt, dich und mich,
nimmt uns zusammen wie ein Bogenstrich,
der aus zwei Saiten eine *Stimme zieht.*
Auf welches Instrument sind wir gespannt?
Und welcher Geiger hat uns in der Hand?
O süsses Lied.

BUDDHA

Als ob er horchte. Stille: eine Ferne . . .
Wir halten ein und hören sie nicht mehr.
Und er ist Stern. Und andre grosse Sterne,
die wir nicht sehen, stehen um ihn her.

O er ist Alles. Wirklich, warten wir,
dass er uns sähe? Sollte er bedürfen?
Und wenn wir hier uns vor ihm niederwürfen,
er bliebe tief und träge wie ein Tier.

Denn das, was uns zu seinen Füssen reisst,
das kreist in ihm seit Millionen Jahren.
Er, der vergisst was wir erfahren
und der erfährt was uns verweist.

it over you to reach to other things?
Oh, I would like to hide it out of sight
with something lost in endless darkenings,
in some remote, still place, so desolate
it does not sing whenever your depth sings.
Yet all that touches us, myself and you,
takes us together like a violin bow
that draws a single voice out of two strings.
Upon what instrument have we been strung?
And who is playing with us in his hand?
Sweet is the song.

BUDDHA

As if he listened. Silence: something far—
we pause but do not hear it anymore.
And he is star. And other mighty stars
that we do not perceive, surround his core.

Oh, he is all. And do we wait indeed
that he might see us? Should he be in need?
Though we dropped to the ground like wind-swept fruit,
he would stay deep and inert as a brute.

For that which tears us down before his feet,
revolves in him for many million years.
He who forgets that which to us appears,
and who beholds what censures our conceit.

DER GEFANGENE

I

Meine Hand hat nur noch eine
Gebärde, mit der sie verscheucht;
auf die alten Steine
fällt es aus Felsen feucht.

Ich höre nur dieses Klopfen
und mein Herz hält Schritt
mit dem Gehen der Tropfen
und vergeht damit.

Tropften sie doch schneller,
käme doch wieder ein Tier.
Irgendwo war es heller–.
Aber was wissen wir.

II

Denk dir, das was jetzt Himmel ist und Wind,
Luft deinem Mund und deinem Auge Helle,
das würde Stein bis um die kleine Stelle
an der dein Herz und deine Hände sind.

Und was jetzt in dir morgen heisst und: dann
und: späterhin und nächstes Jahr und weiter–
das würde wund in dir und voller Eiter
und schwäre nur und bräche nicht mehr an.

Und das was war, das wäre irre und
raste in dir herum, den lieben Mund
der niemals lachte, schäumend von Gelächter.

Und das was Gott war, wäre nur dein Wächter
und stopfte boshaft in das letzte Loch
ein schmutziges Auge. Und du lebtest doch.

THE PRISONER

I

My hand is left but one
gesture with which it wards off;
on the ancient stone
it drips as into a trough.

I only hear how it knocks,
and my heart keeps pace
as it drips on the rocks
and leaves no trace.

That the drops were not so slow,
or another animal came!
Somewhere it was brighter.
But what do we know?

II

Imagine that what now is wind and sky,
air for your mouth and brightness for your eye,
would become stone except for that small part
in which your hands are and your heart.

And what you call Tomorrow now, or Then,
or Later On, Another Year, and thus,
would turn to sores in you and fill with pus
and festered only and would not begin.

And that which was, turned mad and raged around
within you, lips that laughter never crowned,
screaming with laughter, foaming in disorder.

And that which once was God, was but your warder
and plugged, malignant, into the last hole
a dirty eye—but did not take your soul.

DER PANTHER

IM JARDIN DES PLANTES, PARIS

Sein Blick ist vom Vorübergehn der Stäbe
so müd geworden, dass er nichts mehr hält.
Ihm ist, als ob es tausend Stäbe gäbe
und hinter tausend Stäben keine Welt.

Der weiche Gang geschmeidig starker Schritte,
der sich im allerkleinsten Kreise dreht,
ist wie ein Tanz von Kraft um eine Mitte,
in der betäubt ein grosser Wille steht.

Nur manchmal schiebt der Vorhang der Pupille
sich lautlos auf—. Dann geht ein Bild hinein,
geht durch der Glieder angespannte Stille—
und hört im Herzen auf zu sein.

EIN FRAUEN-SCHICKSAL

So wie der König auf der Jagd ein Glas
ergreift, daraus zu trinken, irgendeines,—
und wie hernach der welcher es besass
es fortstellt und verwahrt als wär es keines:

so hob vielleicht das Schicksal, durstig auch,
bisweilen Eine an den Mund und trank,
die dann ein kleines Leben, viel zu bang
sie zu zerbrechen, abseits vom Gebrauch

THE PANTHER

IN THE JARDIN DES PLANTES, PARIS

His glance, worn by the passing of the bars,
has grown so weary it has lost its hold.
It seems to him, there are a thousand bars,
and then behind a thousand bars no world.

The soft gait of the supple, forceful paces,
revolving in a circle almost nil,
is like a dance of power that embraces
a core containing, dazed, a mighty will.

Rarely the pupil's curtain, soundlessly,
is raised—and then an image enters him,
goes through the silent tension of the limbs—
and in his heart ceases to be.

A WOMAN'S FATE

Even as a king may sometimes seize a glass
to drink from it when hunting—any one—
and afterwards the one whose glass it was
puts it away just as if it were none:

so Fate perhaps has sometimes thirsty, too,
raised one up to his eager lips and drunk—
whom, far too anxious, a small life has shrunk
from breaking and has, far from any use,

hinstellte in die ängstliche Vitrine,
in welcher seine Kostbarkeiten sind
(oder die Dinge, die für kostbar gelten).

Da stand sie fremd wie eine Fortgeliehne
und wurde einfach alt und wurde blind
und war nicht kostbar und war niemals selten.

RÖMISCHE FONTÄNE

BORGHESE

Zwei Becken, eins das andre übersteigend
aus einem alten runden Marmorrand,
und aus dem oberen Wasser leis sich neigend
zum Wasser, welches unten wartend stand,

dem leise redenden entgegenschweigend
und heimlich, gleichsam in der hohlen Hand
ihm Himmel hinter Grün und Dunkel zeigend
wie einen unbekannten Gegenstand;

sich selber ruhig in der schönen Schale
verbreitend ohne Heimweh, Kreis aus Kreis,
nur manchmal träumerisch und tropfenweis

sich niederlassend an den Moosbehängen
zum letzten Spiegel, der sein Becken leis
von unten lächeln macht mit Übergängen.

placed on a fragile cupboard's crystal tray
on which it keeps all its most precious finds
(or what is so considered anywhere).

And there she stood, strange as one loaned away,
and simply became old and became blind,
and was not precious and was never rare.

ROMAN FOUNTAIN

BORGHESE

Two basins—and, surpassing, one ascends
out of an ancient, rounded marble band,
and from the upper, water softly tends
to waters that beneath it waiting stand

and meet with silence the soft-speaking friends,
and secretly, as in a hollow hand,
show them the sky where green and darkness ends,
as if it were a new-discovered land;

and, quiet, circle spreads from circle, while
they fill the bowl and feel no homeward longing;
only sometimes some dreamy drops are thronging

over the mossy rim, slide, and repose
on the last level which brings a soft smile
upon the stone beneath with overflows.

ORPHEUS. EURYDIKE. HERMES

Das war der Seelen wunderliches Bergwerk.
Wie stille Silbererze gingen sie
als Adern durch sein Dunkel. Zwischen Wurzeln
entsprang das Blut, das fortgeht zu den Menschen,
und schwer wie Porphyr sah es aus im Dunkel.
Sonst war nichts Rotes.

Felsen waren da
und wesenlose Wälder. Brücken über Leeres
und jener grosse graue blinde Teich,
der über seinem fernen Grunde hing
wie Regenhimmel über einer Landschaft.
Und zwischen Wiesen, sanft und voller Langmut,
erschien des einen Weges blasser Streifen,
wie eine lange Bleiche hingelegt.

Und dieses einen Weges kamen sie.

Voran der schlanke Mann im blauen Mantel,
der stumm und ungeduldig vor sich aussah.
Ohne zu kauen frass sein Schritt den Weg
in grossen Bissen; seine Hände hingen
schwer und verschlossen aus dem Fall der Falten
und wussten nicht mehr von der leichten Leier,
die in die Linke eingewachsen war
wie Rosenranken in den Ast des Ölbaums.
Und seine Sinne waren wie entzweit:
indes der Blick ihm wie ein Hund vorauslief,
umkehrte, kam und immer wieder weit
und wartend an der nächsten Wendung stand—

ORPHEUS. EURYDICE. HERMES

That was the souls' weird mine.
Like silent silver ores they penetrated
as veins its dark expanses. Between roots
welled up the blood that flows on to mankind,
and in the dark looked hard as porphyry.
Else nothing red.

But rock was there
and woods that had no nature. Bridges spanned the void
and that great gray blind pond
suspended over its far distant depth
as rainy skies above a landscape.
And between meadows, soft and full of patience,
appeared the ashen streak of the one way
as a long pallor that has been stretched out.

And it was on this one way that they came.

In front, the slender man in the blue mantle
who looked ahead in silence and impatience.
His paces, without chewing, gulped the way
in outsized swallows; and his hands were hanging
heavy and sullen from the fall of folds,
knowing no longer of the weightless lyre
grown deep into his left as rambler roses
into the branches of an olive tree.
His senses were as if they had been parted:
and while his glances, doglike, ran ahead,
turned back, and came, and always stood again
as waiting at the next turn of the way—

blieb sein Gehör wie ein Geruch zurück.
Manchmal erschien es ihm als reichte es
bis an das Gehen jener beiden andern,
die folgen sollten diesen ganzen Aufstieg.
Dann wieder wars nur seines Steigens Nachklang
und seines Mantels Wind was hinter ihm war.
Er aber sagte sich, sie kämen doch;
sagte es laut und hörte sich verhallen.
Sie kämen doch, nur wärens zwei
die furchtbar leise gingen. Dürfte er
sich einmal wenden (wäre das Zurückschaun
nicht die Zersetzung dieses ganzen Werkes,
das erst vollbracht wird), müsste er sie sehen,
die beiden Leisen, die ihm schweigend nachgehn:

Den Gott des Ganges und der weiten Botschaft,
die Reisehaube über hellen Augen,
den schlanken Stab hertragend vor dem Leibe
und flügelschlagend an den Fussgelenken;
und seiner linken Hand gegeben: sie.

Die So-geliebte, dass aus einer Leier
mehr Klage kam als je aus Klagefrauen;
dass eine Welt aus Klage ward, in der
alles noch einmal da war: Wald und Tal
und Weg und Ortschaft, Feld und Fluss und Tier;
und dass um diese Klage-Welt, ganz so
wie um die andre Erde, eine Sonne
und ein gestirnter stiller Himmel ging,
ein Klage-Himmel mit entstellten Sternen—:
Diese So-geliebte.

his hearing stayed behind him as a smell.
Sometimes it seemed to him as if it reached
back to the walking of those other two
who were to follow him this whole ascent.
Then it was but the echo of his climbing
and his own mantle's wind that was behind him.
Yet he said to himself that they would come;
said it out loud and heard it fade away.
They would come yet, only were two
walking most silently. And if he might
turn only once (and if his looking back
were not destruction of this whole endeavor
still to be ended), he would surely see them,
the quiet two who followed him in silence:

the god of going and of the wide message,
the travel hood shading his brilliant eyes,
bearing the slender staff before his body,
the beat of wings around his ankle bones;
and given over to his left hand: *she.*

The one so loved that from a single lyre
wails came surpassing any wailing women;
that out of wails a world arose in which
all things were there again: the wood and valley
and way and village, field and brook and beast;
and that around this wailing-world, just as
around the other earth, a sun revolved
and a vast sky, containing stars and stillness,
a wailing-sky full of disfigured stars—
this one so loved.

Sie aber ging an jenes Gottes Hand,
den Schritt beschränkt von langen Leichenbändern,
unsicher, sanft und ohne Ungeduld.
Sie war in sich, wie Eine hoher Hoffnung,
und dachte nicht des Mannes, der voranging,
und nicht des Weges, der ins Leben aufstieg.
Sie war in sich. Und ihr Gestorbensein
erfüllte sie wie Fülle.
Wie eine Frucht von Süssigkeit und Dunkel,
so war sie voll von ihrem grossen Tode,
der also neu war, dass sie nichts begriff.

Sie war in einem neuen Mädchentum
und unberührbar; ihr Geschlecht war zu
wie eine junge Blume gegen Abend,
und ihre Hände waren der Vermählung
so sehr entwöhnt, dass selbst des leichten Gottes
unendlich leise, leitende Berührung
sie kränkte wie zu sehr Vertraulichkeit.

Sie war schon nicht mehr diese blonde Frau,
die in des Dichters Liedern manchmal anklang,
nicht mehr des breiten Bettes Duft und Eiland
und jenes Mannes Eigentum nicht mehr.

Sie war schon aufgelöst wie langes Haar
und hingegeben wie gefallner Regen
und ausgeteilt wie hundertfacher Vorrat.

Sie war schon Wurzel

But she walked at the hand of this great god,
her striding straitened by the grave's long wraps,
uncertain, soft, and void of all impatience.
She was in herself as one high in hope,
not thinking of the man who went ahead,
nor of the way ascending into life.
She was in herself. And her having died
filled her as fullness.
And as a fruit is full of dark and sweetness,
the greatness of her death was filling her
and was so new, she comprehended nothing.

She was wrapped up in a new maidenhood
and one not touchable; her sex was closed
as a young flower is toward evening,
and her hands had become so unaccustomed
to matrimony, even the light god's
immeasurably lightly leading touch
offended her as something intimate.

She was not any longer this blond woman
who in the poet's songs would sometimes echo,
not any more the broad bed's scent and island,
and the possession of this man no more.

She was already loosed as flowing hair
and long relinquished as the fallen rain
and meted out as hundredfold provisions.

She was become a root.

Und als plötzlich jäh
der Gott sie anhielt und mit Schmerz im Ausruf
die Worte sprach: Er hat sich umgewendet–,
begriff sie nichts und sagte leise: Wer?

Fern aber, dunkel vor dem klaren Ausgang,
stand irgend jemand, dessen Angesicht
nicht zu erkennen war. Er stand und sah,
wie auf dem Streifen eines Wiesenpfades
mit trauervollem Blick der Gott der Botschaft
sich schweigend wandte, der Gestalt zu folgen,
die schon zurückging dieses selben Weges,
den Schritt beschränkt von langen Leichenbändern,
unsicher, sanft und ohne Ungeduld.

ARCHAÏSCHER TORSO APOLLOS

Wir kannten nicht sein unerhörtes Haupt,
darin die Augenäpfel reiften. Aber
sein Torso glüht noch wie ein Kandelaber,
in dem sein Schauen, nur zurückgeschraubt,

sich hält und glänzt. Sonst könnte nicht der Bug
der Brust dich blenden, und im leisen Drehen
der Lenden könnte nicht ein Lächeln gehen
zu jener Mitte, die die Zeugung trug.

Sonst stünde dieser Stein entstellt und kurz
unter der Schultern durchsichtigem Sturz
und flimmerte nicht so wie Raubtierfelle;

And when with sudden force
the god stopped her and with pain in his cry
pronounced the words: He has turned back—
she comprehended nothing and said softly: Who?

But far off, dark beyond the clear egress,
stood someone, any one, whose countenance
could not be recognized. He stood and saw
how on the pale streak of a meadow path,
with sorrow in his eyes, the god of message
turned silently to follow back the form
that even then returned this very way,
her striding straitened by the grave's long wraps,
uncertain, soft, and void of all impatience.

ARCHAIC TORSO OF APOLLO

We did not know his high, unheard-of head
where his eyes' apples ripened. Yet his torso has
retained their glowing as
a candelabrum where his vision, not yet dead,

only turned low, still shines. For else the breast
could not blind you, nor could we still discern
the smile that wanders in the loins' faint turn
to that core which once carried manhood's crest.

Else would this stone, disfigured and too small,
stand mute under the shoulders' lucid fall,
and not gleam like a great cat's skin, and not

und bräche nicht aus allen seinen Rändern
aus wie ein Stern: denn da ist keine Stelle,
die dich nicht sieht. Du musst dein Leben ändern.

LEDA

Als ihn der Gott in seiner Not betrat,
erschrak er fast, den Schwan so schön zu finden;
er liess sich ganz verwirrt in ihm verschwinden.
Schon aber trug ihn sein Betrug zur Tat,

bevor er noch des unerprobten Seins
Gefühle prüfte. Und die Aufgetane
erkannte schon den Kommenden im Schwane
und wusste schon: er bat um Eins,

das sie, verwirrt in ihrem Widerstand,
nicht mehr verbergen konnte. Er kam nieder
und halsend durch die immer schwächre Hand

liess sich der Gott in die Geliebte los.
Dann erst empfand er glücklich sein Gefieder
und wurde wirklich Schwan in ihrem Schooss.

BUDDHA IN DER GLORIE

Mitte aller Mitten, Kern der Kerne,
Mandel, die sich einschliesst und versüsst,—
dieses Alles bis an alle Sterne
ist dein Fruchtfleisch: Sei gegrüsst.

burst out of all its contours, bright
as a great star: there is no spot
that does not see you. You must change your life.

LEDA

When the god entered him, impelled by need,
he felt the beauty of the swan, amazed;
he vanished into him, frightened and dazed.
Yet his deceit swept him into the deed

before, in his new state, he could have tested
its untried feelings. And, all opened, she
already recognized the deity,
already knew: what he requested,

she, dazed in her defense, could not withstand
nor hide from him. He came down, smooth and white,
and sliding his neck through her weakening hand,

he loosed his godhead in her loveliness—
then only felt his feathers' full delight
and truly became swan in her caress.

BUDDHA IN THE GLORY

Center of all centers, core of cores,
almond, self-enclosed as it grows sweet—
all of this up to all stars
is your fruit flesh: you I greet.

Sieh, du fühlst, wie nichts mehr an dir hängt;
im Unendlichen ist deine Schale,
und dort steht der starke Saft und drängt.
Und von aussen hilft ihm ein Gestrahle,

denn ganz oben werden deine Sonnen
voll und glühend umgedreht.
Doch in dir ist schon begonnen,
was die Sonnen übersteht.

LIED

Du, der ichs nicht sage, dass ich bei Nacht
weinend liege,
deren Wesen mich müde macht
wie eine Wiege.
Du, die mir nicht sagt, wenn sie wacht
meinetwillen:
wie, wenn wir diese Pracht
ohne zu stillen
in uns ertrügen?

Sieh dir die Liebenden an,
wenn erst das Bekennen begann,
wie bald sie lügen.

Du machst mich allein. Dich einzig kann ich vertauschen.
Eine Weile bist dus, dann wieder ist es das Rauschen
oder es ist ein Duft ohne Rest.
Ach, in den Armen hab ich sie alle verloren,
du nur, du wirst immer wieder geboren:
weil ich niemals dich anhielt, halt ich dich fest.

See, you feel how nothing weighs on you;
in the infinite you have your shell,
and there stands the surging sap and brews.
And from outside a vast radiance helps,

for immeasurably above, your suns
are revolving, full and glowing.
Yet in you that has begun
which, when suns are dead, keeps growing.

SONG

You whom I don't tell that I lie awake
at night and weep,
whose being, like a cradle, makes
me tired and tender;
you who don't tell me when for my sake
you cannot sleep:
what if we endured this splendor
and let it ache
without relieving?

Look, when the lovers start
confiding the thoughts of their heart,
how soon they're deceiving.

You make me alone. You only I can exchange.
A while it is you, then a noise that seems strange,
or it is a fragrance without endeavor.
All whom I held in my arms did not remain,
but you are reborn again and again:
because I never held you, I hold you forever.

DIE NEUNTE ELEGIE

Warum, wenn es angeht, also die Frist des Daseins
hinzubringen, als Lorbeer, ein wenig dunkler als alles
andere Grün, mit kleinen Wellen an jedem
Blattrand (wie eines Windes Lächeln)–: warum dann
Menschliches müssen–und, Schicksal vermeidend,
sich sehnen nach Schicksal? . . .

Oh, nicht, *weil Glück* ist,
dieser voreilige Vorteil eines nahen Verlusts.
Nicht aus Neugier, oder zur Übung des Herzens,
das auch im Lorbeer wäre. . . . •

Aber weil Hiersein viel ist, und weil uns scheinbar
alles das Hiesige braucht, dieses Schwindende, das
seltsam uns angeht. Uns, die Schwindendsten. Ein *Mal*
jedes, nur ein *Mal.* Ein *Mal und nichtmehr. Und wir auch*
ein *Mal. Nie wieder. Aber dieses*
ein *Mal gewesen zu sein, wenn auch nur* ein *Mal:*
irdisch *gewesen zu sein, scheint nicht widerrufbar.*

Und so drängen wir uns und wollen es leisten,
wollens enthalten in unsern einfachen Händen,
im überfüllteren Blick und im sprachlosen Herzen.
Wollen es werden.–Wem es geben? Am liebsten
alles behalten für immer . . . Ach, in den andern Bezug,
wehe, was nimmt man hinüber? Nicht das Anschaun, das hier
langsam erlernte, und kein hier Ereignetes. Keins.
Also die Schmerzen. Also vor allem das Schwersein,
also der Liebe lange Erfahrung,–also
lauter Unsägliches. Aber später,
unter den Sternen, was solls: die *sind* besser *unsäglich.*

ELEGY IX

Why, if the span of existence may be completed as
laurel, a little darker than all
other green, with little waves on the
edge of every leaf (like the smile of a wind): why then
have to be human and, dodging destiny,
languish for destiny?

Oh, not because happiness *comes,*
this hasty advantage of an impending loss.
Not for curiosity's sake or to train the heart
which would be in the laurel, too.

But because being here is much, and because apparently
all that is here needs us, all the fleeting that
strangely concerns us. Us, the most fleeting. *Once*
everything, only *once. Once* and no more. And we, too,
once. Never again. But having
been this *once,* even though only *once:*
having been on earth does not seem revokable.

And so we strain and want to accomplish it,
want to contain it in our simple hands,
in still more overcrowded eyes and a speechless heart.
Want to become it. Give it to whom? Would love to
hold on to all forever. Oh, to that other relation,
alas, what can one take across? Not the art of seeing, slowly
learned here, and no event from here. None.
Only our suffering. Only, that is, what was hard;
only the long experience of love—only
what is unsayable. But later,
under the stars, what matter? *They* are rightly unsayable.

Bringt doch der Wanderer auch vom Hange des Bergrands
nicht eine Hand voll Erde ins Tal, die Allen unsägliche, sondern
ein erworbenes Wort, reines, den gelben und blaun
Enzian. Sind wir vielleicht hier, *um zu sagen: Haus,*
Brücke, Brunnen, Tor, Krug, Obstbaum, Fenster,—
höchstens: Säule, Turm. . . . aber zu sagen, *verstehs,*
oh zu sagen so, wie selber die Dinge niemals
innig meinten zu sein. Ist nicht die heimliche List
dieser verschwiegenen Erde, wenn sie die Liebenden drängt,
dass sich in ihrem Gefühl jedes und jedes entzückt?
Schwelle: was ists für zwei
Liebende, dass sie die eigne ältere Schwelle der Tür
ein wenig verbrauchen, auch sie, nach den vielen vorher
und vor den Künftigen. . . ., leicht.

Hier *ist des* Säglichen Zeit, hier *seine Heimat.*
Sprich und bekenn. Mehr als je
fallen die Dinge dahin, die erlebbaren, denn,
was sie verdrängend ersetzt, ist ein Tun ohne Bild.
Tun unter Krusten, die willig zerspringen, sobald
innen das Handeln entwächst und sich anders begrenzt.
Zwischen den Hämmern besteht
unser Herz, wie die Zunge
zwischen den Zähnen, die doch,
dennoch, die preisende bleibt.

Preise dem Engel die Welt, nicht die unsägliche, ihm
kannst du nicht grosstun mit herrlich Erfühltem; im Weltall,

After all, the wanderer from the slope of the mountain, too,
does not bring to the valley a handful of earth, the unsayable, but
some acquired word, pure, the yellow and blue
gentian. Are we perhaps *here* just to say: house,
bridge, well, gate, jug, fruit tree, window—
at most: column, tower—but to *say* it, understand,
oh, to say it as the things themselves never
thought of existing intensely. Is it not the secret cunning
of this taciturn earth when it urges lovers
that in their feeling everything, everything delights?
Threshold: what is it to
two lovers that they wear down their own, already old, threshold
a little, they, too, after the many before them
and before those to come—so slightly.

Here is the time for what is *sayable, here* is its home.
Speak and confess. More than ever
things crumble away that we can experience, for
that which replaces them is imageless action.
Action under crusts that willingly burst as soon as
the activity inside outgrows them and seeks other limits.
Between the hammers endures
our heart, like the tongue
between our teeth that yet
continues to praise.

Praise the world to the Angel, but not the unsayable; him
you cannot impress with the splendor of feelings; out in space

wo er fühlender fühlt, bist du ein Neuling. Drum zeig
ihm das Einfache, das, von Geschlecht zu Geschlechtern
gestaltet,
als ein Unsriges lebt, neben der Hand und im Blick.
Sag ihm die Dinge. Er wird staunender stehn; wie du
standest
bei dem Seiler in Rom, oder beim Töpfer am Nil.
Zeig ihm, wie glücklich ein Ding sein kann, wie schuldlos
und unser,
wie selbst das klagende Leid rein zur Gestalt sich
entschliesst,
dient als ein Ding, oder stirbt in ein Ding–, und jenseits
selig der Geige entgeht.–Und diese, von Hingang
lebenden Dinge verstehn, dass du sie rühmst;
vergänglich,
traun sie ein Rettendes uns, den Vergänglichsten, zu.
Wollen, wir sollen sie ganz im unsichtbarn Herzen
verwandeln
in–o unendlich–in uns! Wer wir am Ende auch seien.

Erde, ist es nicht dies, was du willst: unsichtbar
in uns erstehn?–Ist es dein Traum nicht,
einmal unsichtbar zu sein?–Erde! unsichtbar!
Was, wenn Verwandlung nicht, ist dein drängender
Auftrag?
Erde, du liebe, ich will. Oh glaub, es bedürfte
nicht deiner Frühlinge mehr, mich dir zu gewinnen–,
einer,
ach, ein einziger ist schon dem Blute zu viel.
Namenlos bin ich zu dir entschlossen, von weit her.
Immer warst du im Recht, und dein heiliger Einfall
ist der vertrauliche Tod.

where he feels more feelingly, you are a novice. Therefore show
him what is simple and, molded from generation unto generation,
lives on as ours beside our hands and in our eyes.
Say the things to him. He will stand more astonished—as you stood
before the roper in Rome or the potter in Egypt.
Show him how happy a thing can be, how innocent and how much ours,
how even lamenting grief purely resolves to take form,
serves as a thing or dies into a thing—and escapes beyond
from the violin, blissfully. And these things that live
on destruction understand that you praise them; evanescent,
they trust that we, the most evanescent, can save them.
Wish that we might transform them entirely in our invisible hearts
into—oh, infinite!—into ourselves, whoever we may be.

Earth, is not this what you want: to arise in us
invisible?—Is it not your dream
to be invisible once?—Earth! invisible!
What if not transformation is your urgent command?
Earth, my beloved, I will. Oh, believe me, it requires
your springs no longer to win me for you; one,
alas, even one is already too much for my blood.
Nameless, I am resolved to you from afar.
Always you have been right, and your holy idea
is intimate death.

Siehe, ich lebe. Woraus? Weder Kindheit noch Zukunft
werden weniger. . . . Überzähliges Dasein
entspringt mir im Herzen.

SONETTE AN ORPHEUS: (I, 3)

Ein Gott vermags. Wie aber, sag mir, soll
ein Mann ihm folgen durch die schmale Leier?
Sein Sinn ist Zwiespalt. An der Kreuzung zweier
Herzwege steht kein Tempel für Apoll.

Gesang, wie du ihn lehrst, ist nicht Begehr,
nicht Werbung um ein endlich noch Erreichtes;
Gesang ist Dasein. Für den Gott ein Leichtes.
Wann aber sind *wir? Und wann wendet* er

an unser Sein die Erde und die Sterne?
Dies ists *nicht, Jüngling, dass du liebst, wenn auch*
die Stimme dann den Mund dir aufstösst,—lerne

vergessen, dass du aufsangst. Das verrinnt.
In Wahrheit singen, ist ein andrer Hauch.
Ein Hauch um nichts. Ein Wehn im Gott. Ein Wind.

Behold, I am living. From where? Neither childhood
nor future
grow less.—Superabundant existence
leaps up in my heart.

SONNETS TO ORPHEUS (I, 3)

A god can do it. But how can one follow,
mere man, oh, tell me, through the narrow art?
Man's sense is discord. Where ways of the heart
are crossing stands no temple for Apollo.

Song, as you teach it, does not reach nor yearn,
nor does it woo what is at last attained;
song is existence. For the god, unstrained.
But when do we exist? When will he turn,

to help us to exist, the earth and sky?
It is not this, youth, that you love, although
your voice then opens up your lips—oh, try

forgetting that you ever sang. That flees.
Singing in truth is breath that does not flow.
An aimless breath. Suspense in god. A breeze.

SONETTE AN ORPHEUS: (II, 9)

Rühmt euch, ihr Richtenden, nicht der entbehrlichen Folter
und dass das Eisen nicht länger an Hälsen sperrt.
Keins ist gesteigert, kein Herz–, weil ein gewollter
Krampf der Milde euch zarter verzerrt.

Was es durch Zeiten bekam, das schenkt das Schafott
wieder zurück, wie Kinder ihr Spielzeug vom vorig
alten Geburtstag. Ins reine, ins hohe, ins thorig
offene Herz träte er anders, der Gott

wirklicher Milde. Er käme gewaltig und griffe
strahlender um sich, wie Göttliche sind.
Mehr *als ein Wind für die grossen gesicherten Schiffe.*

Weniger nicht, als die heimliche leise Gewahrung,
die uns im Innern schweigend gewinnt
wie ein still spielendes Kind aus unendlicher Paarung.

SONETTE AN ORPHEUS: (II, 12)

Wolle die Wandlung. O sei für die Flamme begeistert,
drin sich ein Ding dir entzieht, das mit Verwandlungen prunkt;
jener entwerfende Geist, welcher das Irdische meistert,
liebt in dem Schwung der Figur nichts wie den wendenden Punkt.

SONNETS TO ORPHEUS: (II, 9)

Jubilate not when you judge that no rack is required,
men's necks no longer stretched in metallic splendor.
None is enhanced, no man's heart, because a desired
spasm of mildness makes your contortion more tender.

What they received through the ages, the rack and the
rod,
scaffolds surrender as children the toys of their previous
birthday. Into the pure, the high, the undevious,
opened-up heart—thus does not enter the god

of genuine mildness. He would come with might and
expand
radiantly as but the godlike will.
More than a wind for huge ships that are safe near the
land.

Neither less than the secret, silent vibration
conquering us from within like a still
playing child of an infinite copulation.

SONNETS TO ORPHEUS: (II, 12)

Choose to be changed. Oh experience the rapture of fire
in which a life is concealed, exulting in change as it
burns;
and the projecting spirit who is master of the entire
earth loves the figure's flight less than the point where it
turns.

Was sich ins Bleiben verschliesst, schon ists das Erstarrte;
wähnt es sich sicher im Schutz des unscheinbaren Grau's?
Warte, ein Härtestes warnt aus der Ferne das Harte,
Wehe—: abwesender Hammer holt aus!

Wer sich als Quelle ergiesst, den erkennt die Erkennung;
und sie führt ihn entzückt durch das heiter Geschaffne,
das mit Anfang oft schliesst und mit Ende beginnt.

Jeder glückliche Raum ist Kind oder Enkel von Trennung,
den sie staunend durchgehn. Und die verwandelte Daphne
will, seit sie lorbeern fühlt, dass du dich wandelst in Wind.

[FEBRUAR, 1924]

Da dich das geflügelte Entzücken
über manchen frühen Abgrund trug,
baue jetzt der unerhörten Brücken
kühn berechenbaren Bug.

Wunder ist nicht nur im unerklärten
Überstehen der Gefahr;
erst in einer klaren reingewährten
Leistung wird das Wunder wunderbar.

That which would lock itself up—already is frozen.
Does it feel safe in the shadow of colorless gray?
Wait, what is hardest will warn from afar what has chosen
hardness: a hammer will shatter its prey.

He that squanders himself as a well is cognized by cognition
and it leads him rejoicing through the serene creation
which often ceases to start and begins with the end.

Every span of delight is the child or grandchild of division
which they traverse in wonder. And Daphne, since her transformation
into a baytree, desires that you choose to be changed into wind.

[FEBRUARY, 1924]

Winged enchantment bore you through the dark
over many early clefts and ridges,
now construct the boldly reckoned arc
of unheard-of bridges.

Miracle is not just unexplained
weathering of danger;
an achievement, granted and unstrained,
is a miracle far stranger.

Mitzuwirken ist nicht Überhebung
an dem unbeschreiblichen Bezug,
immer inniger wird die Verwebung,
nur Getragensein ist nicht genug.

Deine ausgeübten Kräfte spanne,
bis sie reichen, zwischen zwein
Widersprüchen . . . Denn im Manne
will der Gott beraten sein.

(FÜR HELMUTH FREIHERRN LUCIUS VON STOEDTEN)

Wie die Natur die Wesen überlässt
dem Wagnis ihrer dumpfen Lust und keins
besonders schützt in Scholle und Geäst:
so sind auch wir dem Urgrund unseres Seins
nicht weiter lieb; er wagt uns. *Nur dass wir,*
mehr noch als Pflanze oder Tier,
mit *diesem Wagnis gehn; es wollen; manchmal auch*
wagender sind (und nicht aus Eigennutz)
als selbst das Leben ist—, um einen Hauch
wagender . . . . Dies schafft uns, ausserhalb von Schutz,
ein Sichersein, dort wo die Schwerkraft wirkt
der reinen Kräfte; was uns schliesslich birgt
ist unser Schutzlossein und dass wir's so
in's Offne wandten, da wir's drohen sahen,
um es, im weitsten Umkreis, irgendwo,
wo das Gesetz uns anrührt, zu bejahen.

Toward the indescribable connection
helping is not haughty or omniscient;
as the web increases in affection,
merely being borne is not sufficient.

Stretch your practiced powers like arms of lyres
till they reach, until they span
contradictions.—For the god requires
helpful counsel from the man.

[A DEDICATION OF 1924]

As nature leaves whatever lives to face
the venture of blind pleasure, without freeing
a single one to find a hiding place,
we too are to the ground of our being
in no way dear; it ventures us. Yet still
much more than plant or beast, we will
this venture, move with it, and sometimes even are
more venturous (and not from selfishness)
than even life itself, by a breath more
venturous. . . . This fashions us, though shelterless,
safe dwelling at the core of gravitation
amid pure forces; what brings us salvation
is that, confronted with the threat, we dare
to turn into the open, shelterless,
till in the widest spaces, anywhere,
where the law touches us we may say Yes.

(AUS DEM BRIEFWECHSEL MIT ERIKA MITTERER)

Taube, die draussen blieb, ausser dem Taubenschlag,
wieder in Kreis und Haus, einig der Nacht, dem Tag,
weiss sie die Heimlichkeit, wenn sich der Einbezug
fremdester Schrecken schmiegt in den gefühlten Flug.

Unter den Tauben, die allergeschonteste,
niemals gefährdetste, kennt nicht die Zärtlichkeit;
wiedererholtes Herz ist das bewohnteste:
freier durch Widerruf freut sich die Fähigkeit.

Über dem Nirgendssein spannt sich das Überall!
Ach der geworfene, ach der gewagte Ball,
füllt er die Hände nicht anders mit Wiederkehr:
rein um sein Heimgewicht ist er mehr.

Ragaz, am 24. August 1926

[PROBABLY RILKE'S LAST GERMAN POEM]

(FROM THE CORRESPONDENCE WITH ERIKA MITTERER)

Dove that remained outside,   outside the dovecote,
back in its sphere and home,   one with the day and
night,
it knows the secrecy   when the most remote
terror is fused into   deeply felt flight.

Of all the doves the   always most protected,
never endangered most,   does not know tenderness;
richest of all hearts is   the resurrected;
turning back liberates,   freedom rejoices.

Over the nowhere   arches the everywhere.
Oh, the ball that is   thrown, that we dare,
does it not fill our hands   differently than before?
By the weight of return   it is more.

GEORG TRAKL

(1887-1914)

Born in Salzburg, Trakl studied pharmacy, served for some time as a medical orderly, and then as a civil servant. He was plagued with anxieties, depressions, and despair. In 1913 he took an overdose of Veronal. The person closest to him was his sister, who later ended her own life in 1917. In the army in the early months of the war, he lived through the battle of Grodek, then had to look after ninety severely wounded men whom he felt unable to help. He attempted suicide, was taken to a military hospital for observation, and died of an overdose of cocaine.

He himself published several volumes but was content only with his little collection of *Gedichte* (1913) and *Sebastian im Traum* (1914, Sebastian in a Dream). Much material was published only posthumously.

Ludwig Wittgenstein, the Viennese philosopher who eventually became a professor at Cambridge University in England, at one time made large financial gifts, anonymously, to help Rilke and Trakl, but preferred Trakl's verse because he found him less pretentious. Martin Heidegger, whose Rilke interpretation has been mentioned, has also published an essay on "Georg Trakl" in the periodical, *Merkur* (Stuttgart, March 1953). The shortcomings of this exegesis have been analyzed by Walter Muschg, professor of German literature at Basel, in *Die Zerstörung der deutschen Literatur* (1956, The Destruction of German Literature), in the tragicomic chapter "Zerschwatzte Dichtung." The comic touch is supplied by the quotations from Heidegger and his minions.

In English, little has been written on Trakl, but Michael Hamburger's *Reason and Energy: Studies in German Literature* (1957) contains a chapter on Trakl as well as essays on Hölderlin, Novalis, Heine, and Benn, to mention only poets represented in this volume. Although the Trakl interpretation takes issue with Heidegger on some points, it quite fails to prick Heidegger's bubble as Muschg did, who is not mentioned, and the whole discussion moves more or less on Heidegger's plane and in places approximates what Muschg calls "Zerschwatzte Dichtung"—poetry chattered to bits. Consider a few of Hamburger's comments on Trakl's "Lament," one of the three poems that follow.

"What is important is that the poem deals with two different disasters. The first . . . is that 'eternity's icy wave would or may swallow' the 'golden image of man'; that is to say, that men will be untrue to their Creator beyond all possibility of redemption." The critic goes on to admit immediately "that 'eternity's icy wave' is not a Christian concept; but Trakl, after all, had read Nietzsche, . . . and his despair was bound to be coloured by the current modes of unbelief . . . In order to express his despair—a conditional despair—he had to resort to the language of unbelief . . ."

The exegete's "that is to say" is reminiscent of a preacher reading his thought for the week into an all but unrelated text. The moody vagueness and allusiveness of the poet's melancholy images are sacrificed to theological clichés; the absence of anything Christian is explained away along with the presence of admittedly un-Christian concepts; and in case we are not persuaded by the critic's strong claim that the images of unbelief were "bound to" enter, we are told once more that Trakl "had to resort to the language of unbelief."

"Since boats symbolize existence, the sinking boat of the tenth line has the effect of a final disaster." Is it no disaster when boats sink that do not symbolize existence? But the worst is yet to come: "One would be inclined to read a reference to Trakl's own death into these lines, if the tone of the poem were not so impersonal." Indeed one would; and if one can put out of one's mind the critic's theology, the poem ceases to be impersonal.

Three pages before all this (on p. 263), Trakl's sister has been spirited out of the poem: "The 'sister' of other late poems . . . although not a hermaphrodite in herself, . . . is the feminine complement of the poet's masculine spirit. The absurdity of identifying this sister with Trakl's sister Margarete is evident from his last poem, in which it is the sister's shade that appears; and Trakl's sister was neither dead at the time . . . nor actually present on the battlefield." Evident indeed! Is it not cricket for a poet to think of the person closest to him as coming toward him unless she is either dead or actually present? Of course, Michael Hamburger is an able poet and translator, and there is much to be learned from the volume cited. The passages quoted are representative not of the book as a whole but only of its very worst pages—and of much Trakl interpretation. That is the reason for citing them here: to give some idea of Trakl's reception by the critics—a story almost as melancholy as the poet himself, but not without involuntary humor.

Perhaps Trakl tended, a little like Eichendorff in this respect, to write the same poem over and over again. But his poem is not so innocuous and least of all contrived: it is an anguished vision, a deeply personal outcry. And instead of letting Trakl's lament speak straight to the heart and mind, too many critics have buried it under the icy wave of pretentious interpretations.

Trakl's poems are collected in his *Gesammelte Werke*, Otto Müller Verlag, Salzburg, and the three that follow are reproduced with the publisher's kind permission.

UNTERGANG

AN KARL BORROMÄUS HEINRICH

Über den weissen Weiher
Sind die wilden Vögel fortgezogen.
Am Abend weht von unseren Sternen ein eisiger
Wind.

Über unsere Gräber
Beugt sich die zerbrochene Stirne der Nacht.
Unter Eichen schaukeln wir auf einem silbernen
Kahn.

Immer klingen die weissen Mauern der Stadt.
Unter Dornenbogen
O mein Bruder klimmen wir blinde Zeiger gen
Mitternacht.

RUH UND SCHWEIGEN

Hirten begruben die Sonne im kahlen Wald.
Ein Fischer zog
In härenem Netz den Mond aus frierendem Weiher.

In blauem Kristall
Wohnt der bleiche Mensch, die Wang' an seine Sterne
gelehnt;
Oder er neigt das Haupt in purpurnem Schlaf.

UNTERGANG

Over the white pond
the wild birds have flown away.
From our stars blows in the evening an icy
wind.

Over our graves
the broken brow of the night bends down.
Under oaktrees we rock in a silver
skiff.

Always the white walls of the town resound.
Under bows of thorns
O my brother we climb, blind hands, toward
midnight.

REST AND SILENCE

Shepherds buried the sun in the bare forest.
A fisherman hauled
in a hairy net the moon from a freezing pond.

In blue crystal
dwells the pallid man, his cheek leaning against his stars;
or he inclines his head in crimson sleep.

Doch immer rührt der schwarze Flug der Vögel
Den Schauenden, das Heilige blauer Blumen,
Denkt die nahe Stille Vergessenes, erloschene Engel.

Wieder nachtet die Stirne in mondenem Gestein;
Ein strahlender Jüngling
Erscheint die Schwester in Herbst und schwarzer
Verwesung.

KLAGE

Schlaf und Tod, die düstern Adler
Umrauschen nachtlang dieses Haupt:
Des Menschen goldnes Bildnis
Verschlänge die eisige Woge
Der Ewigkeit. An schaurigen Riffen
Zerschellt der purpurne Leib.
Und es klagt die dunkle Stimme
Über dem Meer.
Schwester stürmischer Schwermut
Sieh ein ängstlicher Kahn versinkt
Unter Sternen,
Dem schweigenden Antlitz der Nacht.

Yet always the black flight of the birds moves
the visionary, the sacred of blue blossoms,
the near stillness thinks what is forgotten, extinguished
angels.

Again the brow sleeps in moonish stone;
a radiant youth,
the sister appears in autumn and black decay.

LAMENT

Sleep and death, the gloomy eagles,
roar all night around this head:
that the golden image of man
is devoured by the icy wave
of eternity. On eerie cliffs
the crimson body is smashed.
And the dark voice is lamenting
over the sea.
Sister of stormy melancholy,
see an anxious skiff sink
under stars,
the silent face of the night.

FRANZ WERFEL

(1890-1945)

◇◇

Werfel was born in Prague, like Rilke. He attended the old university there, also studied in Leipzig and Hamburg, and on the eve of World War I was an editor in Kurt Wolff's publishing house. He was a soldier during the war, then went to Berlin, later to Vienna. He married the widow of Gustav Mahler, the composer. Being a Jew, he emigrated to France in 1938, and hence to the United States where he spent the last five years of his life.

His international reputation was built on his novels, which were widely translated. Probably the best known of these, though not necessarily the best, is *Das Lied der Bernadette* (1941, The Song of Bernadette), which was made into a very popular motion picture. Among his plays, *Jacobowsky und der Oberst* (1943) gained a worldwide success when it was filmed under the title, *Me and the Colonel,* starring Danny Kaye and Curt Juergens.

His poetry is not nearly so well known, but literary historians consider him the most important lyric poet of German expressionism. And *The Oxford Book of German Verse* (2nd edition, 1927) concludes with the poem reprinted here—of course, only in German. This sonnet may well be his finest poem. It was originally published in the collection *Wir sind* (1913, We Are), and is reprinted here with the kind permission of S. Fischer Verlag, Frankfurt am Main.

ALS MICH DEIN WANDELN AN DEN TOD VERZÜCKTE

Als mich dein Dasein tränenwärts entrückte,
Und ich durch dich ins Unermessne schwärmte,
Erlebten diesen Tag nicht Abgehärmte,
Mühselig Millionen Unterdrückte?

Als mich dein Wandeln an den Tod verzückte,
War Arbeit um uns und die Erde lärmte.
Und Leere gab es, gottlos Unerwärmte,
Es lebten und es starben Niebeglückte!

Da ich von dir geschwellt war zum Entschweben,
So viele waren, die im Dumpfen stampften,
An Pulten schrumpften und vor Kesseln dampften.

Ihr Keuchenden auf Strassen und auf Flüssen!
Gibt es ein Gleichgewicht in Welt und Leben,
Wie werd ich diese Schuld bezahlen müssen!?

WHEN YOU ENRAPTURED ME

When my eyes filled, by your presence possessed,
and thanks to you I soared through the untold,
was not that day felt by the sick and old,
by millions that were cruelly oppressed?

When you enraptured me till death seemed best,
toil was around us, noise, decay, and mold,
and emptiness, and godless ones were cold;
men lived and died that never had been blessed.

When you had swelled me till my senses swirled
and I could fly, the musty dark was teeming,
at desks men shriveled, and the mills were steaming.

You that on roads and rivers chafe and fret:
if there is any balance in the world,
how shall I have to pay this guilty debt?

GOTTFRIED BENN

(1886-1956)

Benn studied medicine at the University of Berlin and became a doctor. *Morgue* (1912), his first collection of verse, came out as he absolved his military service. A few days later, April 9, 1912, his mother died of cancer. Later the same year, Benn published his poem about the cancer ward in a periodical. During the War, while he was in the service, all five of the poems that follow appeared along with some of his other verse in a little book with the title *Fleisch* (translatable as either Flesh or Meat)—the third volume in a new series of *Aktions-Lyrik* (Action Poetry).

It is very doubtful whether any of Benn's later verse ever equaled the power and originality of these early poems. They were not his first. When he was 18, he had submitted some of his poems to a journal that offered to review anonymously submitted verse, and after a few weeks received the verdict: "G.B.—friendly in outlook, weak in expression." But he never published his juvenilia. His late verse (1937–1955) is considered his best by some German critics; and the fact that some of his late poems are unimpressive does not constitute a refutation: Goethe, for example, also wrote many unimportant poems. But even the poems most highly regarded by some of Benn's admirers are deficient in originality: they are all too similar to the late verse of Rilke, particularly to such poems as the two of 1924 that are included in this volume. Some are also modeled after the late wisdom poems of Goethe, occasionally to the point of only slightly varying some of Goethe's lines.

Benn's name has always been associated with his early poems. Whether one thinks of Auschwitz as one reads them or whether one considers them early harbingers of existentialism, one can hardly deny their shocking power which is far greater than that of most beatnik poetry. There are at least two reasons for this.

First, these poems do not conform to a familiar pattern; they are not just another example of something that many others had done before or were doing at the same time. What shocks is the brutal honesty of an unprecedented perception. Like Kierkegaard and Nietzsche, and unlike the existentialists after World War I and the beatniks after World War II, Benn's early verse is *unzeitgemäss* (untimely)—prophetic rather than fashionable.

Secondly, these poems, like Benn's late verse, are highly disciplined and do not spend their force in repetitions or invective. It is not surprising that Nietzsche should have been one of Benn's heroes. One is reminded of Nietzsche's fine phrase, "the economy of the great style"; of Nietzsche's remark, "it is my ambition to say in ten sentences what everyone else says in a book—what everyone else does *not* say in a book"; and of Nietzsche's contempt for poetry that is "too popular—a mere garrulity of feelings" (*Twilight of the Idols,* 1889, in *The Portable Nietzsche,* 556f.).

In 1950 Benn wrote an essay on Nietzsche (included

in the first volume of his *Gesammelte Werke*, 1959): "Really everything discussed by my generation, thought through in our minds—one could say: suffered through; one could also say: spun out [*breittrat*]—all that has already been expressed and exhausted by Nietzsche; he had given the definitive formulations, all the rest was exegesis. His dangerous, tempestuous, lightninglike manner, his restless diction, his denying himself every idyl and every universal ground, his positing of a psychology of drives, of a man's constitution as a motif, of physiology as a dialectic—'knowledge as an affect,' the whole of psychoanalysis, the whole of existentialism—all this is his deed. He is, as becomes ever more apparent, the far-reaching giant of the post-Goethean epoch. Now some people come and say that Nietzsche is politically dangerous. Now one really should consider politicians in this perspective. They are people who, when they become rhetorical, always hide behind the theses of men whom they do not understand—men of the spirit. . . . Nietzsche saw that coming. . . . The blond beast that materialized he would certainly not have welcomed. He, as a human being, was poor and pure—a great martyr and man. I might add: for my generation he was the earthquake of the epoch and since Luther the greatest master of the German language [*das grösste deutsche Sprachgenie*]."

The German word *breittreten* is much more picturesque than "spin out": it means stepping on something, especially a joke or a fine point, and thus flattening it out, spoiling it by overelaboration. Compare Christian Morgenstern's "The Economical Poet" and "The Glasses," above.

Benn's remarks about Nietzsche and the Nazis are doubly noteworthy because he might easily have been tempted to cite Nietzsche in extenuation of his own reception of Hitler. But what he did say is in line with the verdict of all informed students of Nietzsche's works.

In 1931 Benn had delivered and printed a celebrated speech in honor of Heinrich Mann. In 1933, after Hitler had taken over Germany, Benn received an open letter from Thomas Mann's son, Klaus, from France: ". . . you—as indeed the *only* German author our kind had counted on—have *not* resigned from the Academy. . . . What could induce you to put your name—to us a byword for high standards and an all but fanatical purity—at the disposal of men whose lack of standards is unmatched in European history and from whose moral squalor the world recoils? . . . What friends can you gain on so wrong a side? . . . Heinrich Mann, whom you worshipped as no one else, has been shamefully kicked out of the same organization you're staying in. . . . You, of course, must know what you get in exchange for our love . . . ; unless I'm a bad prophet, it will eventually be ingratitude and derision." In reply, Benn published his *Antwort an die literarischen Emigranten* (Reply to the Literary Emigrants) in a little book, *Der neue Staat und die Intellektuellen* (1933, The New State and the Intellectuals). A translation of this "Reply" may be found in *Primal Vision: Selected Writings of Gottfried Benn* (1958), edited by E. B. Ashton, from whose introduction parts of Klaus Mann's letter have been quoted here. In his "Reply" Benn said, in italics: "I do not belong to the Party, have no relationship to its leaders, and I do not count on new friends."

But he also made clear that he was quite taken in by Hitler's propaganda, and for a few months he and some of his essays were considered very useful and given considerable publicity by the government. Before the end of 1934 he was *persona non grata,* and in 1935 he went back into the German army, as a doctor, defining his course as "an aristocratic form of emigration."

On May 7, 1936, a few days after his fiftieth birthday, *Das Schwarze Korps,* the newspaper of the S.S., addressed him "*Du Schwein*" (you swine); and by 1938 he was officially forbidden to publish. His comeback after the War began with the publication in Switzerland of *Statische Gedichte* (1948, Static Poems), and during the following decade his fame grew steadily.

The poems that follow are reprinted with the kind permission of Limes Verlag, Wiesbaden, publisher of Benn's *Gesammelte Werke.*

MORGUE

SCHÖNE JUGEND

Der Mund eines Mädchens, das lange im Schilf gelegen hatte,
sah so angeknabbert aus.
Als man die Brust aufbrach, war die Speiseröhre so löcherig.
Schliesslich in einer Laube unter dem Zwerchfell
fand man ein Nest von jungen Ratten.
Ein kleines Schwesterchen lag tot.
Die andern lebten von Leber und Niere,
tranken das kalte Blut und hatten
hier eine schöne Jugend verlebt.
Und schön und schnell kam auch ihr Tod:
Man warf sie allesamt ins Wasser.
Ach, wie die kleinen Schnauzen quietschten!

KREISLAUF

Der einsame Backzahn einer Dirne,
die unbekannt verstorben war,
trug eine Goldplombe.
Die übrigen waren wie auf stille Verabredung ausgegangen.
Den schlug der Leichendiener sich heraus,
versetzte ihn und ging für tanzen.
Denn, sagte er,
nur Erde solle zur Erde werden.

BEAUTIFUL CHILDHOOD

The mouth of a girl who had lain long in the reeds
looked so gnawed at.
When one broke open the breast, the esophagus was so
full of holes.
Finally in a bower under the diaphragm
one found a nest of young rats.
One little sister lay dead.
The others were living on liver and kidney,
drank the cold blood and had
spent a beautiful childhood here.
And beautiful and fast their death, too, came:
One threw the lot of them into the water.
Oh, how the little snouts squeaked!

CYCLE

The lonely molar of a whore
who had died unknown
had a filling of gold.
The others, as if they had a silent understanding,
had gone out.
That one the morgue attendant knocked out,
marketed, and went dancing.
For, he said,
only earth shall return to earth.

NEGERBRAUT

Dann lag auf Kissen dunklen Bluts gebettet
der blonde Nacken einer weissen Frau.
Die Sonne wütete in ihrem Haar
und leckte ihr die hellen Schenkel lang
und kniete um die bräunlicheren Brüste,
noch unentstellt durch Laster und Geburt.
Ein Nigger neben ihr: durch Pferdehufschlag
Augen und Stirn zerfetzt. Der bohrte
zwei Zehen seines schmutzigen linken Fusses
ins Innere ihres kleinen weissen Ohrs.
Sie aber lag und schlief wie eine Braut:
am Saume ihres Glücks der ersten Liebe
und wie vorm Aufbruch vieler Himmelfahrten
des jungen warmen Blutes.
Bis man ihr
das Messer in die weisse Kehle senkte
und einen Purpurschurz aus totem Blut
ihr um die Hüften warf.

NEGRO BRIDE

Then, bedded upon pillows of dark blood,
the blond neck lay of a white woman.
The sun was raging in her hair
and licked the length of her light thighs
and kneeled around the slightly browner breasts,
that neither vice nor birth had yet disfigured.
A nigger next to her: by a horse's hoof
his eyes and forehead shredded. He dug
two toes of his dirty left foot
into the inside of her small white ear.
Yet she lay sleeping like a bride:
on the edge of the joys of her first love,
as on the eve of many an Ascension
of the warm youthful blood.
Until one plunged
the knife into her white throat, throwing
a crimson apron of dead blood
around her hips.

MANN UND FRAU GEHN DURCH DIE KREBSBARACKE

Der Mann:
Hier diese Reihe sind zerfallene Schösse
und diese Reihe ist zerfallene Brust.
Bett stinkt bei Bett. Die Schwestern wechseln stündlich.

Komm, hebe ruhig diese Decke auf.
Sieh, dieser Klumpen Fett und faule Säfte,
das war einst irgendeinem Manne gross
und hiess auch Rausch und Heimat.

Komm, sieh auf diese Narbe an der Brust.
Fühlst du den Rosenkranz von weichen Knoten?
Fühl ruhig hin. Das Fleisch ist weich und schmerzt nicht.

Hier diese blutet wie aus dreissig Leibern.
Kein Mensch hat so viel Blut.
Hier dieser schnitt man
erst noch ein Kind aus dem verkrebsten Schoss.

Man lässt sie schlafen. Tag und Nacht.—Den Neuen
sagt man: Hier schläft man sich gesund.—Nur sonntags
für den Besuch lässt man sie etwas wacher.

Nahrung wird wenig noch verzehrt. Die Rücken
sind wund. Du siehst die Fliegen. Manchmal
wäscht sie die Schwester. Wie man Bänke wäscht.

Hier schwillt der Acker schon um jedes Bett.
Fleisch ebnet sich zu Land. Glut gibt sich fort.
Saft schickt sich an zu rinnen. Erde ruft.

MAN AND WOMAN WALK THROUGH THE CANCER WARD

The man:
Here this row is disintegrated wombs,
and this row is disintegrated breast.
Bed stinks by bed. Nurses change hourly.

Come, do not hesitate to lift this blanket.
Look here, this lump of fat and putrid juices,
this once was great for some man somewhere
and was called ecstasy and home.

Come, look here at this scar on that breast.
You feel that rosary of softened knots?
Don't hesitate. The flesh is soft and hurts not.

Here this one bleeds as if from thirty bodies.
No human has such quantities of blood.
From this a child
had to be cut first from her cancerous womb.

One lets them sleep. Both day and night.—The new ones
are told: here one sleeps oneself healthy.—Only Sundays,
for visitors, they're left a little more awake.

They do not take much nourishment. Their backs
are sore. You see the flies. Sometimes
the nurses wash them. As one washes benches.

Here the field swells already round each bed.
Flesh becomes almost soil. Ardor is spent.
Juices prepare to flow. The earth is calling.

SAAL DER KREISSENDEN FRAUEN

Die ärmsten Frauen von Berlin
—dreizehn Kinder in anderthalb Zimmern,
Huren, Gefangene, Ausgestossene—
krümmen hier ihren Leib und wimmern.
Es wird nirgends so viel geschrien.
Es wird nirgends Schmerzen und Leid
so ganz und gar nicht wie hier beachtet,
weil hier eben immer was schreit.

„Pressen Sie, Frau! Verstehn Sie, ja?
Sie sind nicht zum Vergnügen da.
Ziehn Sie die Sache nicht in die Länge.
Kommt auch Kot bei dem Gedränge!
Sie sind nicht da, um auszuruhn.
Es kommt nicht selbst. Sie müssen was tun!“
Schliesslich kommt es: bläulich und klein.
Urin und Stuhlgang salben es ein.

Aus elf Betten mit Tränen und Blut
grüsst es ein Wimmern als Salut.
Nur aus zwei Augen bricht ein Chor
von Jubilaten zum Himmel empor.

Durch dieses kleine fleischerne Stück
wird alles gehen: Jammer und Glück.
Und stirbt es dereinst in Röcheln und Qual,
liegen zwölf andere in diesem Saal.

LABOR ROOM

The poorest women of Berlin
—in a room and a half they expect thirteen—
prisoners, outcasts, whores,
writhe here and sob.
Nowhere else is there so much screaming.
Nowhere else is suffering and pain
something one so completely ignores
because here something always screams.

"Bear down, woman! Understand? Bear down!
You did not come here to have fun.
Don't draw it out. Don't just wait.
Push even if you evacuate!
You are not here to get a rest.
It does not come by itself. You have to press!"
At last it comes: small and somewhat blue,
anointed with urine and feces, too.

From eleven beds of tears and blood
sobbing greets it as a salute.
A choir rises from only two eyes
to bear jubilation to the skies.

Through this little hunk of flesh here all
will pass in time: delight and gall.
And once it dies rattling and meets its doom,
others will fill the twelve beds in this room.

KLABUND

(1890-1928)

◇◇

His first poems, sponsored by Alfred Kerr, a highly perceptive and influential critic, netted him a lawsuit, on a charge of blasphemy. He won and was famous. His real name was Alfred Henschke, but his fame has always been tied to his pseudonym.

He published several volumes of verse and some passionate and powerful novels, including *Moreau* (1915), *Mohammed* (1917), *Pjotr* (1923, the story of Peter the Great), *Rasputin* (1928), and *Borgia: Roman einer Familie* (1928, Borgia: The Novel of a Family). He also wrote a brief history of world literature that has been very widely read, and some unsurpassed recreations of Japanese and, above all, Chinese poems. His version of a Chinese play, *Der Kreidekreis* (1924, The Chalk Circle) became especially popular and helped to inspire Bertold Brecht's drama, *Der kaukasische Kreidekreis* (1949). Perhaps his versions of Chinese lyric poems (collected in *Chinesische Gedichte: Nachdichtungen, Gesamtausgabe*) have enriched German literature as much as anything he wrote: the more one reads rival versions, whether in German or in English, the more impressive they seem.

Like Rilke before him and George after him, he died

in Switzerland—but in the German-speaking part, at Davos, of consumption. He was buried where he had been born, at Krossen on the Oder; and Gottfried Benn spoke, recalling how they had gone to school together and been friends for twenty-five years.

The poems that follow are reprinted by courtesy of Phaidon Press, London.

ALLES, WAS GESCHIEHT

Alles, was geschieht,
Ist nur Leid und Lied.
Gott spielt auf der Harfe Trost sich zu,
Welle fällt und steigt.
Ach wie bald schon neigt
Sich dein Haupt im Tod. Dann lächle du.

WAFFENSPRUCH (TSÜI-TAO)

Wie ihr den Bogen spannt—so spannt auch eure Seele!
Besorgt, dass nicht der Pfeil zu kurz geschnitten werde . . .
Zielt bei Attacken auf die Pferde!
Seht, dass ihr eure Feinde lebend fangt—und lebend ihre Generäle . . .

Tut alles recht im Zweck, so muss es euch gelingen.
Was nützt es, tagelang im Blute waten?
Es ziele euer Ruhm: den Feind zu z w i n g e n .
Ihr seid keine Mörder. Ihr seid Soldaten.

RITT

Der Schimmel raucht. Wie Hunde springen braun
Wälder an mir empor. Der Tempel. Fromm
Geläut des Morgens. Schräge Sonne hängt
Wie Blendlaterne in getrübter Luft.

ALL THAT COMES TO BE

All that comes to be
is pain and poetry.
God plays on the harp to soothe his grief.
Waves fall and ascend.
Ah how soon you bend
your head in death. Then smile relief.

AFTER TSUI-TAO

As you must strain the bow, thus strain your souls and strive
to cut a long and deadly sharpened arrow.
In battle aim to pierce the horses' marrow.
See that you catch your enemies unharmed and all their generals alive.

Serve righteously the cause, and you will overthrow.
What good to wade in blood by day and night?
Your glory is to *force* the foe.
You shall not murder. You shall fight.

RIDE (AFTER AN UNKNOWN CHINESE POET)

The horse is foaming. Like dogs brown
forests jump at me. The temple. Pious
morning bells. The sun suspended like
a brilliant lantern in the misty air.

O welches Glück, auf einem Tier zu sein
Und Flügel haben an dem Ackergold!
Ein Pfeil. Ich falle hell. Zweibeinig steigt
Das Pferd ins Licht. In seinen leeren Augen
Steht das Entsetzen wie ein schwarzer Turm.

WINTERKRIEG (LI-TAI-PE)

Ich träume von dem Regenbogen
Und den Gärten meiner Heimat Thsin.
Mimosen blühen gelb. Gazellen hüpfen.
Wohl ist Krieg. Aber Krieg von Sonne warm.

Wir frieren mit den Pferden am Wege fest.
Manchem werden eiserne Beine abgeschnitten.
In den Stiefeln. Augen erfrieren wie Glas.
Wohl dem, der unterm Schneeweiss schläft, zu Tod gebräunt.

Wir Bettler. Unsre Kleider sind zerfetzt.
Fels starrt wie Eis, und Eis starrt wie Gestein.
In Spiralen dreht sich zuckend des Pass.
Hündisch klettern wir den Mond hinauf.

Wie Maulbeerborke platzt die Haut.
Unser eignes Blut rinnt aufs Schwert.
Hörner klingen in dumpfer Qual.
Süsser sang ich zur Flöte einst.

Keiner Heimkehr bin ich mir bewusst.
Ein Tiger, aufgescheucht, schlägt mit dem Schweif,

Infinite joy to be on horseback now
with wings outspread while all the fields are golden!
An arrow. I fall sharply. The horse ascends
two-legged into the light. And in his empty eyes
stands horror like a tower, black.

WINTER WAR (AFTER LI PO)

I dream of the rainbow
and of the gardens of my homeland.
Mimosas bloom yellow. Gazelles are leaping.
There is war. But war warm with sun.

On our horses we freeze fast to the road.
Some have their legs cut off, iron.
In their boots. Eyes freeze like glass.
Blessed are those who sleep under snow, tanned to death.

We beggars. Our clothes in shreds.
Rocks glare like ice. And ice like stone.
Trembling in spirals turns the mountain pass.
Doglike we climb the moon.

Like bark our skin cracks.
Our own blood drips on our swords.
Horns sound in muted agony.
Sweeter I sang to the flute once.

I know of no return.
A tiger, awakened, beats the snow with his tail,

Fletscht seine Zähne, weiss wie Reif, und dunkel
Rollt sein brüllender Ruf ins Tal.

Zeige jemand sein Herz! Vogel fällt vom Baum.
Trete hervor und zeige sein Herz. Wo ist rot ein Herz?
Tannen stehn beschneit, und auf den Zweigen
Hocken wir steif und krähn im Nebel des Bluts.

O Himmel! Heiliger! Hilf, verbrenne mich!
Lass Wintergewitter grau erdonnern–und wirf
Den Blitz in die erstarrt erhobene Stirne,
Dass ich aufsteige, Feuersäule, in Nacht.

bares his teeth, white like frost, but dark
rolls his thundering roar to the valley.

Show someone his heart. A bird falls from a tree.
Step out and show his heart. Where is, red, a heart?
Fir trees stand snowed in, and on the branches
we crouch stiff and caw in a mist of blood.

O heaven! Holy one! Help! Burn me!
Let winter storms thunder up gray and cast
lightning on my frozen raised-up forehead
that I ascend, a pillar of fire in the night.

ERICH KÄSTNER

(BORN 1899)

Kästner was born in Dresden. He was 15 when World War I broke out, but old enough to participate before it was over. After the War he studied German literature and received his doctorate. He began his literary career as an editorial writer for a newspaper in Leipzig, but later went to Berlin to make his living as a writer. Between 1927 and 1932 he published four volumes of verse. The first two poems that follow come from *Ein Mann gibt Auskunft* (1930, A Man Gives Information); the last is taken from *Gesang zwischen den Stühlen* (1932, Song Between the Chairs). In 1959 his *Gesammelte Schriften in Sieben Bänden* (Collected Works in Seven Volumes) appeared, and the first volume contains all of his verse, including *Kurz und Bündig: Epigramme* (1948, expanded edition 1950; Brief and Pithy: Epigrams).

Kästner's most successful book appeared in 1928: *Emil und die Detektive* (Emil and the Detectives). Like many of the best children's books, it proved equally appealing to grown-ups; it was made into a play, filmed, and translated into at least twenty languages. Of his many other books for children, *Pünktchen und Anton* (1929, *Pünktchen* is the nickname of a girl) is perhaps the most brilliant; but other readers may well prefer another volume. Both books, as well as Kästner's poems, blend humor with serious moral concerns and are not lacking in pedagogic intent. Kästner has never been afraid to deal with the most serious matters with a light touch, and he has never hidden his abundant wit under a bushel. Neither has he been afraid to be a moralist in an age in which that was distinctly not fashionable. The title of his bitterest book is *Fabian: Die Geschichte eines Moralisten* (1931, Fabian: The Story of a Moralist), and in a postscript, published later, the author keeps insisting that he is a moralist.

He was 33 when Hitler came to power. Besides his novel and his four volumes of verse, he had published a play and five children's books. He had left no doubt where he stood. Twenty-four years later, in 1957, when he received the Georg Büchner Prize (awarded to Benn in 1951), Kästner said: "In May 1933 the book burning took place, and among the twenty-four names selected by the minister for literary cremation to articulate his hatred mine was included. I was strictly forbidden to publish anything further in Germany. During the following years I was arrested twice, and until the collapse of the dictatorship I was under surveillance," being "undesirable and politically unreliable."

He was actually in Switzerland in 1933 and need not have returned to Germany, and the following year a Nazi official asked him whether he might not like to settle down in Switzerland "to found a journal against the emigrants, with secret German state funds. I realized that his views regarding the relation of talent and character were even more rigorous than mine. On the basis of his experiences in the ministry, he evidently thought that talent and character were mutually incompatible as a matter of principle." Kästner believes that "there always have been and are talented people who are nevertheless decent human beings"; and his career helps to prove him right.

During the Nazi years, Kästner was allowed to publish books abroad, provided they passed German censorship. He published several children's books in Zurich; three of his books were filmed; and he made a selection from his verse, omitting the "offensive" poems included here, under the title *Doktor Erich Kästners Lyrische Hausapotheke* (1936, Doctor Erich Kästner's Lyrical Home Pharmacy). After World War II he resumed publication in Germany, mainly in the same genres as before. He also published two comedies, the second under the title *Die Schule der Diktatoren* (1956, The School of the Dictators); two volumes entitled *Chansons und Prosa;* and *Als ich ein kleiner Junge war: Kindheitserinnerungen* (1957, When I Was a Small Boy: Childhood Reminiscences). In the last named book he speaks of his mother in a manner that throws light on his portraits of Emil's and Anton's mothers in his two most popular children's books: "Therefore I became the best pupil and son. I had to become the perfect son. . . . After all, I found the hastily scribbled notes when I came home from school! They lay on the kitchen table. 'I can't go on any more!' they said. 'Don't look for me!' they said. 'Farewell, my dear boy!' they said. And the apartment was empty and cold. . . . Almost always I found her . . . on one of the bridges. . . . " Kästner's life, like that of most good satirists, has not been easy. What saved him again and again was surely his wonderful sense of humor.

The poems that follow are reprinted by permission of the author and Atrium Verlag Zurich. They are also included in Kästner's *Bei Durchsicht meiner Bücher*, copyright Atrium Verlag Zurich.

DIE ANDRE MÖGLICHKEIT

Wenn wir den Krieg gewonnen hätten,
mit Wogenprall und Sturmgebraus,
dann wäre Deutschland nicht zu retten
und gliche einem Irrenhaus.

Man würde uns nach Noten zähmen
wie einen wilden Völkerstamm.
Wir sprängen, wenn Sergeanten kämen,
vom Trottoir und stünden stramm.

Wenn wir den Krieg gewonnen hätten,
dann wären wir ein stolzer Staat.
Und pressten noch in unsern Betten
die Hände an die Hosennaht.

Die Frauen müssten Kinder werfen.
Ein Kind im Jahre. Oder Haft.
Der Staat braucht Kinder als Konserven.
Und Blut schmeckt ihm wie Himbeersaft.

Wenn wir den Krieg gewonnen hätten,
dann wär der Himmel national.
Die Pfarrer trügen Epauletten.
Und Gott wär deutscher General.

Die Grenze wär ein Schützengraben.
Der Mond wär ein Gefreitenknopf.
Wir würden einen Kaiser haben
und einen Helm statt einem Kopf.

THE OTHER POSSIBILITY

If we had won the war with waving
of flags and roaring, if we had,
then Germany would be past saving,
then Germany would have gone mad.

One would attempt to make us tame
like savage tribes that one might mention.
We'd leave the sidewalk if a sergeant came
and stand attention.

If we had won the war of late
we'd be a proud and headstrong state
and press in bed in our dreams
our hands to our trouser seams.

Women must bear, each woman serves
a child a year. Or calaboose.
The state needs children as preserves,
and it swills blood like berry juice.

If we had won the war, I bet
that heaven would be national,
the clergy would wear epaulets,
God be a German general.

Trenches would take the place of borders.
No moon, insignia instead.
An emperor would issue orders.
We'd have a helmet and no head.

Wenn wir den Krieg gewonnen hätten,
dann wäre jedermann Soldat.
Ein Volk der Laffen und Lafetten!
Und ringsherum wär Stacheldraht!

Dann würde auf Befehl geboren.
Weil Menschen ziemlich billig sind.
Und weil man mit Kanonenrohren
allein die Kriege nicht gewinnt.

Dann läge die Vernunft in Ketten.
Und stünde stündlich vor Gericht.
Und Kriege gäb's wie Operetten.
Wenn wir den Krieg gewonnen hätten—
zum Glück gewannen wir ihn nicht.

RAGOUT FIN DE SIECLE

(IM HINBLICK AUF GEWISSE LOKALE)

Hier können kaum die Kenner
in Herz und Nieren schauen.
Hier sind die Frauen Männer.
Hier sind die Männer Frauen.

Hier tanzen die Jünglinge selbstbewusst
im Abendkleid und mit Gummibrust
und sprechen höchsten Diskant.
Hier haben die Frauen Smokings an
und reden tief wie der Weihnachtsmann
und stecken Zigarren in Brand.

If we had won, then everyone
would be a soldier; the entire
land would be run by goon and gun,
and all around would be barbed wire.

On order, women would throw twins,
for men cost hardly more than stone,
and above all one cannot win
a war with guns alone.

Then reason would be kept in fetters,
accused and always on the spot.
And wars would come like operettas.
If we had won the last war—but
we were in luck and we did not.

RAGOUT FIN DE SIÈCLE

(WITH REFERENCE TO CERTAIN CAFÉS)

Here even experts can
hardly see clear:
the women are men,
the men are women here.

Young men are dancing here with zest
in evening dress with rubber breast
while talking in sopranos.
The women wear tuxedos
and talk like Santa Claus
while lighting big Havanas.

Hier stehen die Männer vorm Spiegel stramm
und schminken sich selig die Haut.
Hier hat man als Frau keinen Bräutigam.
Hier hat jede Frau eine Braut.

Hier wurden vor lauter Perversion
Vereinzelte wieder normal.
Und käme Dante in eigner Person—
er frässe vor Schreck Veronal.

Hier findet sich kein Schwein zurecht.
Die Echten sind falsch, die Falschen echt,
und alles mischt sich im Topf,
und Schmerz macht Spass, und Lust zeugt Zorn,
und Oben ist unten, und Hinten ist vorn.
Man greift sich an den Kopf.

Von mir aus, schlaft euch selber bei!
Und schlaft mit Drossel, Fink und Star
und Brehms gesamter Vögelschar!
Mir ist es einerlei.

Nur, schreit nicht dauernd wie am Spiess,
was ihr für tolle Kerle wärt!
Bloss weil ihr hintenrum verkehrt,
seid ihr noch nicht Genies.

Na ja, das wäre dies.

The men go to the powder room
to put cream on their hide.
No woman here has any groom,
each woman has a bride.

Here some tried so hard for perversion
that they returned to the norm.
And if Dante came here on excursion
he would take chloroform.

Here nobody knows what is what.
The true are false, the false are not,
and all is mixed up in a pot,
and pain is fun, pleasure makes mad,
and up is down, and front behind.
One simply goes out of one's mind.

For all I care, have an affair
with yourselves or a mastodon,
or every bird in Audubon.
I do not give a damn.

Only don't scream ad nauseam
that you are great.
That you prefer it from behind
does not prove an ingenious mind.

So much for that.

LEGENDE, NICHT GANZ STUBENREIN

Weihnachten vergangnen Jahres
(17 Uhr präzise) war es:
Dass der liebe Gott nicht, wie gewöhnlich,
den Vertreter Ruprecht runterschickte,
sondern er besuchte uns persönlich.
Und erschrak, als er die Welt erblickte.

Er beschloss dann doch, sich aufzuraffen.
Schliesslich hatte er uns ja geschaffen!
Und er schritt (bewacht von Detektiven
des bewährten Argus-Institutes,
die, wo er auch hinging, mit ihm liefen)
durch die Städte und tat nichts als Gutes.

Gott war nobel, sah nicht auf die Preise,
und er schenkte, dies nur beispielsweise,
den Ministersöhnen Dampfmaschinen
und den Kindern derer, die im Jahre
mehr als 60 000 Mark verdienen,
Autos, Boote—lauter prima Ware.

Derart reichten Gottes Geld und Kasse
abwärts bis zur zwölften Steuerklasse.
Doch dann folgte eine grosse Leere.
Und die Deutsche Bank gab zu bedenken,
dass sein Konto überzogen wäre.
Und so konnte er nichts weiter schenken.

LEGEND, NOT QUITE HOUSEBROKEN

Last year's Christmas Eve at five
Santa Claus did not arrive.
God dispensed with his old substitute,
feeling he himself ought to be calling.
Breaking custom, he stooped to commute
and, arriving, found the world appalling.

But he felt he must not make a fuss:
after all, he had created us.
And he went (well guarded by detectives,
Pinkerton's whom no firm supersedes,
men who followed him to all objectives)
through the towns, did nothing but good deeds.

God was liberal and did not ration,
and he gave, to give an illustration,
steam engines to sons of politicians,
and to those whose fathers earned enough,
boats and cars with up-to-date transmissions.
Prices he ignored, gave first-rate stuff.

God's funds were sufficient, and the racket
did not stop till through the surtax bracket.
Suddenly, a gap began to yawn;
and his bank informed him: Do not spend
any more, account is overdrawn.
So the present-giving had to end.

Gott ist gut. Und weiss es. Und wahrscheinlich
war ihm die Geschichte äusserst peinlich.
Deshalb sprach er, etwa zehn Minuten,
zu drei sozialistisch eingestellten
Journalisten, die ihn interviewten,
von der Welt als bester aller Welten.

Und die Armen müssten nichts entbehren,
wenn es nur nicht so sehr viele wären.
Die Reporter nickten auf und nieder.
Und Gott brachte sie bis ans Portal.
Und sie fragten: „Kommen Sie bald wieder?"
Doch er sprach: „Es war das letzte Mal."

God is good. And knows it. So he sighed
and presumably felt mortified.
He consented to an interview
with three journalists who heard him tell—
they were of a socialistic hue—
that this world was the best possible.

And the poor need not forego a thing
if their numbers were not towering.
The reporters nodded embarrassed, and then
God took them to the golden door.
They asked: Will you come soon again?
But he replied: No, nevermore.

HERMANN HESSE

(BORN 1877)

Like Benn, Hesse is the son of a German minister and a mother of (French) Swiss descent. He was born in Calw, near Stuttgart; his mother, in Farther India. His maternal grandfather was a missionary like his father but also an Orientalist. From his third to his ninth year, Hesse lived in Basel. His family had hoped that he would become a minister, but he worked off and on in bookstores. In 1911 he traveled to India. When World War I broke out, he was in Switzerland, where he decided to stay permanently. He moved to Montagnola, in the Italian part of Switzerland, in 1919, and became a Swiss subject in 1923. He was elected to the Prussian Academy of Poets in 1926, but resigned five years later. In 1946 he won the Nobel Prize for literature.

His career as a poet began with *Romantische Lieder* (1899), but his name became known chiefly through his novels; especially *Peter Camenzind* (1904), *Gertrud* (1910), *Rosshalde* (1914), and *Knulp* (1915). During World War I he suffered a profound personal crisis, from which he emerged as a writer of European stature. In 1919 he published an essay, *Zarathustras Wiederkehr* (Zarathustra's Return); a short story, *Klein und Wagner;*

and, under the pseudonym of Emil Sinclair, his greatest novel up to that time, *Demian.* It was awarded a prize, as a first novel, which Hesse returned, admitting his authorship. *Demian* marked a new beginning. Hence the road led to the short story, *Klingsors letzter Sommer* (1920, Klingsor's Last Summer); to *Siddharta* (1922); *Steppenwolf* (1927); *Narziss und Goldmund* (1930, translated as *Death and the Lover*); *Die Morgenlandfahrt* (1932, translated as *Journey to the East*); and *Das Glasperlenspiel* (1943, translated as *Magister Ludi,* later also as *The Bead Game*).

In 1952, when Hesse's *Gesammelte Dichtungen* were published in seven volumes, his poems were collected, along with some of his prose, in volume 5. The poem that follows and concludes this book was written a few years before World War I, but it is certainly not dated by any of Hesse's later work.

The poem is reprinted with the kind permission of Suhrkamp Verlag, Berlin und Frankfurt am Main.

ALLEIN

Es führen über die Erde
Strassen und Wege viel,
Aber alle haben
Dasselbe Ziel.

Du kannst reiten und fahren
zu zwein und zu drein,
Den letzten Schritt musst du
Gehen allein.

Drum ist kein Wissen
Noch Können so gut,
Als dass man alles Schwere
Alleine tut.

ALONE

All over the earth are roads
and more ways than man has kenned,
but all of them have
the identical end.

You can ride or travel
with two or three,
the last step you take
without company.

Hence nothing better
has ever been known
than that all that is hard
is done alone.